Daily Mail

The Daily Mail Book of
STARTING A FRANCHISE

EVALUATION OF A FRANCHISE

When assessing a franchise, the following considerations should be carefully borne in mind:

1. The product should be a proven one and not merely an idea. It should be well established and possibly known to the public. It should not be a short term fad or fashion.

2. Will the product or service still be in demand in 5 or 10 years time? Is there a company Research and Development programme?

3. Have patents or trade marks been registered?

4. What is the market competition? How flexible are prices against cost of manufacture? Remember that the presence of competition proves there is a market for the product.

5. There must be a sound and established source of supply.

6. Although a business is well established, the franchise operation may be a new concept. Has a pilot scheme been operated and fully evaluated?

7. An in-depth examination of the franchisor as to:
   a. financial standing
   b. up-to-date company accounts
   c. projected cash flow analysis for new franchisees
   d. projected trading account analysis
   e. results from existing franchisees
   f. the resources to support the proposed franchise expansion programme.

8. Who fixes price levels? Franchisor or franchisee? Is there sufficient flexibility?

9. Talk with existing franchisees. Is the franchise all it promises to be?

10. Have there been any failures and what is the franchisor's method of franchisee selection?

11. Is there an Operations Manual available to all franchisees?

12. Is there a management service fee, or royalty, or mark-up on goods supplied? There should be only one source of profit for the franchisor. An average royalty is 10%.

13. Is there a national advertising levy? Does the franchisor match franchisee contributions? Is this levy an additional amount or part of the general royalty?

14. Although a front-end fee is usually charged, it should not be considered a source of profit, but merely an attempt to recoup a franchisor's investment in research and development, legal costs and expenses of the franchise.

15. **The Agreement**
This should be examined by a solicitor. Every Agreement should be considered against the following points:
   a. ensure that there is sufficient flexibility to allow the franchisee to make a reasonable profit
   b. if leasehold premises are used, does the term of years tie in with the period of the Agreement? The Agreement should be established for a sensible period to allow the business to prosper. An average of 3-5 years is usual and automatically renewed when the franchisee is successful
   c. does the franchisor have the right to buy-back?
   d. under what circumstances can the Agreement be terminated and at what cost?
   e. upon sale is goodwill compensated or is it lost by the franchisee?

16. In a seasonal business, can repayment of funding arrangements be met through the year?

17. What term of years is needed to pay back initial investment? Does this include funding?

18. If territories are granted, are these adequate to expand the business? Is registration required under the Restrictive Trade Practices Act at the Office of Fair Trading?

19. There should be no aspect of pyramid selling, as this is now illegal.

20. Exactly what can the franchisor do for a franchisee that a self employed person could not do for himself?

21. Are your family in full agreement with your wish to become self-employed?

If we can be of
any further help,
ring the
Franchise Helpline,
01-356 1795.

Lloyds Bank
Small Business
Services

The Daily Mail Book of STARTING A FRANCHISE

HOW TO START AND RUN A SUCCESSFUL FRANCHISE

Tony Attwood

Harmony Books Ltd
Unit 11, Stirling Industrial Centre, Borehamwood, Herts, WD6 2BT

First published 1990
© Tony Attwood

British Cataloguing in Publication Data
Attwood, Tony
The Daily Mail book of starting a franchise.
1. Great Britain. Franchising
I. Title
658.8'708'0941

ISBN 1 85553 003 1

Designed by Design 29, Dyfed. Typeset by Joachim Holmes
Printed and bound in Great Britain.

ACKNOWLEDGEMENTS
Special thanks to Bolton Agnew of Practical Used Car Rental for the information which his franchise always provides so willingly.
And to Len Hough, co-editor of THE GOOD FRANCHISE GUIDE

AUTHOR'S NOTE
At several points in this book reference is made to the law of the land (for example in terms of an employee's rights) and its implications (in terms of taxation etc). While every care has been taken to ensure the accuracy of what is written, it must be stressed that this is not a legal manual, and in many cases legal positions are given only in outline. It is not impossible for specific instances of the law in operation to be quite different from the general principles outlined here. Furthermore changes may be made to any law at any time, while in some situations the position for businesses operating or registered in Scotland may be quite different from those in the rest of the United Kingdom. It should therefore be clear that the legal information given in this book is for general guidance only and higher authorities should always be consulted for clarification on any specific point.

Throughout the book a number of examples are given of the work of individual franchisors and franchisees. In almost every case these represent invented individuals and companies - Alan Smith, Michael Thomas, Amazingly Fast Printers, Megavan and Universal Metals do not exist in real life and are not intended to represent individuals or companies. Practical Used Car Rentals, Master Thatcher and Dyno Rod, are however genuine franchises.

Tony Attwood
Northamptonshire. October 1989

ABOUT THE AUTHOR
Tony Attwood is co-editor of THE GOOD FRANCHISE GUIDE and author of a number of business books. He runs his own company in Northamptonshire where he lives with his wife and three daughters.

Calling all insurance professionals who want to be No.1 on the High Street

Swinton Insurance, Britain's largest high street insurance specialist, wants to hear from ambitious, forward-thinking professionals who are interested in a highly successful future as a Swinton Franchisee.

With over 500 computerised branches already to our name and a £3.5 million marketing budget at our disposal, the most dynamic source of insurance cover nationwide has plenty to talk about.

Write now for full details in confidence to:
Mr. P.W. Lowe, Franchise Director, Swinton Insurance, Swinton House, 6 Great Marlborough Street, Manchester M1 5SW. Tel: 061-236 1222.

SWINTON INSURANCE

THE INSURANCE FRANCHISE

OUR NAME IS YOUR PROMISE OF SUCCESS.

CONTENTS

CONTENTS

CHAPTER 1

WHAT IS A FRANCHISE?

KEY WORDS DEFINED

All forms of business activity have their own key words which flow freely from the tongues of those in the know, and leave newcomers floundering. Here are the main words and phrases that you have to come to terms with in franchising if you are to understand fully what is going on.

BFA	The British Franchise Association. There are several groupings and associations relating to franchising, of which this is the most well-known and most highly respected. Most major franchises belong to the BFA.
FRANCHISE	The general term for the actual business that is franchised - as in the phrase "Practical Used Car Rental is a franchise".
FRANCHISEE	The person who operates the franchise in one particular area. Large franchises may have up to several hundred franchisees in the UK. So John Smith, who operates the Practical Used Car Rental franchise in one part of London is a franchisee.
FRANCHISOR	The company owning the whole franchising operation. Practical Used Car Rental has its head office in Birmingham, and if you wish to buy the

right to run a Practical franchise you approach the franchisor in Birmingham.

MANUAL   All the franchisor's instructions on how to operate the franchise successfully are contained in the Operations Manual, which is a highly confidential document, only supplied to actual franchisees. How clearly it is written, how well it is indexed, and how comprehensive its instructions are major factors in relation to the success or failure of the franchise.

MASTER FRANCHISE   A franchise licence enabling the operator to handle the franchising for one major area. Typically an American franchisor might offer a master franchise for the UK, the master franchisee then locating and handling franchisees throughout the UK.

PILOT   The trial-run of a franchise. A reputable franchisor will set up a pilot scheme, running the business as a franchisee would, in order to make sure that the idea does work, before he starts offering the franchise to franchisees.

ROYALTY   Franchisees pay the franchisor a regular sum for the right to operate the franchise. This sum may be paid monthly or annually, and may be calculated as a percentage of turnover or as a fixed fee. If the franchise involves selling goods supplied by the franchisor there may be no royalty as such since the franchisor is making a profit on each product sold on to the franchisee.

TERRITORY   The area within which the franchisee is allowed to operate. This is most commonly defined by postcodes, county boundaries or Yellow Pages areas.

Alan Smith was made redundant at the age of 35, taking his redundancy payment and using it to buy a village shop not far from where he lived.

The shop had, in his opinion, been poorly run for some years; the previous owners, taking the view that the locals would buy from the shop come what may, had decided that there was no need to spend money making the shop a particularly attractive place. Nor did they feel any need to go out of their way to offer a quality service: from time to time they were late opening the shop; on Bank holidays it failed to arrange paper deliveries; and generally it did little to endear itself to the locals.

As a result some villagers took to doing their shopping in the next village. In addition a number of touring vans had started visiting the area selling fruit and vegetables, renting out videos and so on. Trade in the village shop declined. Eventually the shop was sold for little more than the value of the property.

Alan decided to reverse this trend from the moment he took over. He went out of his way to ask local villagers what they wanted in their shop, and as soon as he was able he started touring the county visiting other village shops and noting what they sold and how they treated their customers.

Through his work Alan reached the conclusion that many village shops were under-achieving, and he had the idea that once he had got his own shop running as he wanted it, he would consider taking on a second.

As time went by Alan succeeded in his task, doubling the takings in the shop, and increasing the annual profit by 50% in just one year. The outward appearance of the shop was brightened up giving it a style and decor that made it stand out. Alan changed the range of foods that were sold, pulling out of some of the more traditional lines and including some new health products. He even rejuvenated the traditional notice-board which carried postcards advertising second-hand prams for sale and offering work to baby sitters and nannies, by adding drawings from the children in the village school to the display. All the parents looked at the window to see if their child's work was on display.

At the end of two years Alan's village shop looked bright and cheerful; utterly different from the one he had taken over. People now travelled from other villages to buy, rather than the reverse. Alan installed his assistant as manager of his first shop and bought the lease on another some ten miles away. This time he turned the business around in one year rather than two, duplicating the successes of his first shop while avoiding the problems.

By now Alan had an even clearer idea of what made his shops successful. They were both in villages dominated by well-to-do commuters for whom price was not a major concern, who would be more likely to buy health food than canned food and who valued a reliable service above everything else.

But Alan ran into a problem as he looked for a third shop to take over. The next village which fitted the profile he had devised was thirty-five miles away. The thought of the 70-mile round trip each day made him reluctant to develop the shop himself, and yet he felt he did not know anyone who would be able to undertake the work without his guidance. And so Alan turned to franchising. Alan Smith became the franchisor and his first two shops became the pilot studies. He now started seeking a franchisee who would actually be the owner of the third shop, but would develop it by following Alan's proven method. Alan would be spared the cost of setting up the business, and would know that the manager installed in the new shop would be very keen and dedicated to the job - he would after all be the shop's owner, and have everything to gain through increased sales and growing profits. In return Alan would get a royalty income from the franchised shop. Of course there were many who looked at Alan's franchise and thought, "what's the point in paying for a franchise? I know how to run a shop," but in return for his royalty Alan offered a massive amount of support: training, promotional ideas, low prices for bulk buying and an approach already proven as a success.

This story is typical of the way in which a franchise can start. Franchises can be based around ideas (as in Alan's case for a brighter type of village shop which catered for a particular type of client), particular products (for example pizzas, hamburgers, ice creams, clothes), services (such as rapid printing, picture-framing and so on), or a unique patented piece of machinery (such as a machine that cleans out walls prior to re-pointing). Many of the 500 or so franchises on offer in the UK are household names - Alfred Marks, Practical Used Car Rental, Sketchley Dry Cleaning, Prontaprint, Pizza Hut, Late Late Supershop, Dyno-Rod - there are very few areas of business that are not available as franchises.

WHAT DO ALL FRANCHISES HAVE IN COMMON?

Despite the diversity of franchises available, most franchises do have the following factors in common:

1. A license to operate in a certain location. This normally means that no other license will be granted by the franchisor within the same area.

ADVANTAGE:
Reduces but does not normally eliminate opposition. There is nothing to stop another franchise (or a non-franchised company) from setting up in opposition next door to you.)

DISADVANTAGE:

If successful you may wish to expand, but there will often be no opportunity for opening up a second branch nearby, unless another franchise territory remains vacant.

2.   The right to use the franchise's name, logo, and style of presentation.

ADVANTAGE:

If the franchise is already well-known, people will treat the new outlet as a welcome extension of a known firm.

DISADVANTAGE:

If anything goes wrong at headquarters, every franchisee suffers.

3.   The right to operate the franchise for a set period of time.

ADVANTAGE:

You know you have your exclusive territory for enough time to make it worth your while, especially if you also have the right to renew the franchise later if you wish.

DISADVANTAGE:

You may wish to sell up a year or two before your licence runs out, but the business will decline in value if the franchise has only a short period to run, unless a new owner can get an extension both to the franchise and the premises.

4.   The benefit of setting up your business after one or more pilot operations have been run.

ADVANTAGE:

The pilot operations are trial runs which show that the business can be profitable, and should weed out difficulties and problems before the franchisee starts trading.

DISADVANTAGE:

None, if the pilot is truly representative of the way the franchises will work - but remember the pilot only shows that the franchise could work - It does not prove that it will work.

5. Training. - Unless you are entering a business field with which you are totally familiar you will benefit from being trained in everything from selling, to filling-in VAT returns, from actually doing the job at the heart of the franchise (be it printing, car valeting or anything else) to looking after staff.

ADVANTAGE:
You may already know some of this, but the chance to meet with people who have experienced what you are setting out to do and who can pass on tips can be very, very valuable.

DISADVANTAGE:
None if the training is well organised and run by people who are experienced in running this sort of business.

6. The manual - The manual contains the secrets of the franchise - a good manual will tell you everything you need to know from day one to the day you retire.

ADVANTAGE:
When on your own you can often find yourself unsure of how to proceed - the manual should give you answers to questions you don't even know you should be asking.

DISADVANTAGE:
Some manuals are badly written, poorly indexed and difficult to follow; this can be a particular problem when you need guidance on one particular topic in a hurry.

7. **Support in** raising finance - Banks keep records on all franchises and are often more willing to lend to franchisees than to businessmen and women setting up on their own. Likewise if there are leases to be arranged the franchisor may be able to put you in touch with a leasing company that will rapidly arrange the finance you require.

ADVANTAGE:
Raising finance is time consuming and can lead to disappointment especially if your bank manager doesn't appreciate what you are trying to do. The franchisor should supply your bank with profit

forecasts and other financial figures which can save you hours of detailed and often difficult work.

DISADVANTAGE:

There are cases of banks being too keen to lend you money. A small number of very large franchises have crashed, in all cases with the banks still offering to lend money to new franchisees right up until the last moment. Remember that just because a bank offers you money it does not mean that you are bound to be successful.

7. **Set-up help.** - This can range from undertaking some preliminary advertising for you to obtaining the best terms for a lease on the best premises available.

ADVANTAGE:

Some of these preliminaries are time consuming and need expertise just when you don't have it - before you have started in business.

DISADVANTAGE:

You have to pay for this help in your franchise fee whether you use it or not.

8. **Back-up services** - When you have a problem the solution should only be a phone call away.

ADVANTAGE:

When setting up in business the time to solve complex problems is the one thing you do not have.

DISADVANTAGE:

Again you have to pay for the existence of this service even if you don't use it. But beware, not all back-up services are as good as they should be.

9. **Supply of consumables** - All businesses need a variety of consumables from materials used in the actual business process (cleaning materials for a house valeting service, photographic plates for a print shop) through to consumables such as envelopes, business cards, photocopier paper and so on which every business needs.

ADVANTAGE:
Sorting out exactly what you require, finding the best deal and arranging supplies can be time consuming and expensive if you make a mistake.

DISADVANTAGE:
Some franchisors like to make a profit on the consumables they sell on, and this can lead to franchisees paying more for products than necessary.

10. **Other franchisees** - You can talk to other franchisees, compare notes, discuss problems and evaluate successes.

ADVANTAGE:
Setting up and running a business is a lonely affair and the chance of someone to talk to who understands exactly what you are up to is certainly worth while.

DISADVANTAGE:
None - it is always helpful to be able to compare notes with others in the same line of work.

11. **Profit and risk** - Profit projections and budget forecasts should be clearly established from the start by the franchisor so that you should always know exactly where you are going as well as what you have already achieved. The risk of things going wrong should be reduced.

ADVANTAGE:
Being unsure of just how profitable you are (and how profitable you ought to be) is one of the major problems of many small businesses. With a franchise you ought to know exactly where you are going, and how far along the road you have gone. The forecasts and projections should remove some of the risks from the business, since others will have trod this way before and ironed out most of the problems.

DISADVANTAGE:
All reductions in risk have to be paid for - if you are an inveterate gambler you don't need to reduce risks by going for a franchise. But if you don't like a flutter you can consider the franchise royalty part of your insurance against risk.

WHAT'S IN IT FOR THE FRANCHISOR?

We have considered various ways in which a franchise arrangement could be beneficial to a person wanting to start in business for the first time. But what of the franchisor - what is in it for him?

Franchising is first and foremost a way of expanding rapidly without major investment. Once the pilot schemes are running at a profit, the manual is written, the training process is ready and the support team is in place, franchising ought to offer a reasonably simple way of expanding for a firm. (In fact franchisors always complain that it is never as straightforward as it sounds with some franchisees taking up a disproportionate amount of time as they telephone head office with every problem no matter how trivial.)

Nevertheless once a franchise is advertised there tends to be a large number of would-be franchisees knocking on the door, which makes the recruitment of branch owners much easier than it would be if one was simply trying to find local managers.

Franchisees should (in theory at least) make excellent managers, for two reasons. Firstly they should know the local conditions in which the business is to be set up, and secondly they have every incentive to make the business work since it is theirbusiness. They have put up the money, the losses and gains will be theirs. For the franchisee there is the advantage of running one's own business minus some of the risks. For the franchisor there is the opportunity of expansion at reduced costs.

PAYING FOR A FRANCHISE

This is a complex business for the costs of franchising are divided into several separate parts and it is easy to make a miscalculation and underestimate the amount you will have to pay in setting up and running the business. Make sure you take account of all the factors listed below.

FRANCHISE FEE

The franchise fee is an initial payment made by the franchisee to the franchisor for the right to operate the franchise. The fee buys the rights to the manual, other information, back-up and other support, the use of the name and the initial training programme (although not the cost of travelling to the training services, nor the accommodation fees while there).

OTHER SPECIFIED PAYMENTS

What the franchise fee does not buy is the equipment and supplies you need to start trading. You may need to obtain a lease on a shop (with the first three months' rent paid in advance). There will be specialist equipment (ovens to cook the pizza in for example), shopfittings, vehicles and so on. These payments may be far in excess of the cost of the franchise fee.

SETTING UP AND MAINTAINING STANDARDS

The franchise agreement will oblige you to run the business to a particular standard. Since the public sees each franchised outlet as part of a national chain it is important that the standards are always maintained throughout the network. A franchisor will not allow you to cut corners by starting with low grade equipment; you have to open with all guns blazing from day one which means installing all equipment and employing staff straight away.

ROYALTY PAYMENTS

Once you start running the business the franchisor may require you to pay him part of your turnover - 10% is a typical figure although it can be much higher. It is worth emphasising that this percentage is normally based on your turnover, not your profit. If you are running a business with a turnover of half a million pounds you could find yourself paying out £50,000 a year in royalties. And this will be in addition to the money paid out in franchise fee at the start of the operation.

As an alternative some franchises ask for standing payments which are maintained irrespective of the turnover. This has the advantage to the franchisor of making money easier to collect, and to the franchisee of being held at a standard level even when turnover is high. They have the disadvantage of being fixed, even when business is bad.

ADVERTISING FUND

Some franchises operate an advertising fund which is collected separately from the royalty payment, although it too is normally based on a percentage of turnover. The advertising fund is often not asked for every month but instead is called in when a national advertising campaign is required. Franchisees may be represented on the committee that handles the fund so that they can represent franchisee opinion. Look carefully at any franchise which has an advertising fund but no representation from franchisees, and ensure that you are happy with the way the fund (which is money collected from you) is being spent.

COMPULSORY PURCHASES

Franchisees often do not have the freedom to buy regular supplies as and when they like - they have to purchase some, or in some cases all the items required from the franchisor. This may be a great advantage for in theory the franchisor has great buying power and ought to be getting the items at a low price. But it can be annoying if you find the same items for sale down the road at a price less than you are paying.

A GUARANTEED WAY TO MAKE MONEY?

So far we have considered the advantages and disadvantages of franchising. What should be clear from this is that although in some circumstances franchising is a safer way of making money than setting up entirely on your own, franchising is no more guaranteed to be profitable than any other sort of business. If you take on a franchise and it does not make you the money you expect the franchisor is unlikely to give you your fees back. The franchise remains your business and it is up to you to make it work through hard graft, business acumen and determination. However it is true that well established franchises tend to fail less often than other forms of new business, and it is worth understanding why this happens.

Many figures are quoted for the failure rates of new businesses - often ranging from 50 to 70% for failures within the first three years. Whether these figures are true or not is a matter for debate - there is after all no register of businesses save for the details of limited companies left at Companies House, and many of these are set up with no intention that they should ever make a profit.

The helpful guide "How to Evaluate a Franchise", published by the British Franchise Association (BFA) suggests that the failure rate of VAT registered businesses within the first five years of registration is 37%. The difference between this and higher figures quoted elsewhere is probably explained by the fact that many fail before they even achieve VAT registration. The BFA go on to quote a failure rate for newly established franchisees working under reputable franchisors of no more than 3 or 4%.

This makes franchising look astonishingly attractive, but as with all statistics, a little caution is needed. The BFA figures (which you will see widely quoted in franchise prospectuses) relate to established franchises which are recognised by the BFA. If you are looking at a franchise which is not recognised by the BFA, or if you are being more adventurous and considering a franchise that is not well established and at present only has a handful of franchisees, you cannot expect the low failure rate statistic to apply.

Obviously all legitimate franchisors want failure as little as the franchisees, and the reputable franchisor takes great pains to ensure that its selection of franchisees leads to as small a number of problems as possible. Indeed it is not unknown for only very small numbers of franchisees to be selected from hundreds or thousands of original applicants. For example Master Thatchers, the thatching service franchise that won a special commendation in the Franchisor of the Year award in 1989, accepts under 5% of those people who apply for the franchise, and have been known to accept only one applicant in a year.

Other franchises paint a similar picture although the ways in which franchisors de-select hopeful franchisees vary. Master Thatcher invite all applicants for franchises onto a one-week practical course, during which many find the romantic image of sunshine and cottages rapidly diminishing amidst the reality of tall ladders and rain. Such franchisees de-select themselves - and many franchisors report that the number of applicants who come through the various screening processes and then have to be rejected by the franchisor is very small. Practical Used Car Rental, the respected motor trade franchise, report a similar state of affairs, although they allow de- selection by applying a policy of active encouragement only to those individuals whom they feel could be particularly beneficial to the franchise network. Those over whom they have doubts tend to de-select themselves and like Master Thatcher, Practical Use Car Rental rarely have to turn people down.

These selection processes clearly help ensure that the number of franchisees whose businesses fail is very small. Yet it does not take too much imagination to see that a franchisor who does not have such a vigorous screening process may allow all sorts of highly willing but also highly unsuitable franchisees to get through. Under such circumstances the very low failure rate quoted by the BFA will not apply, for it is the screening and de-selection process that effectively reduces the failure rate rather than the mere fact that the business is franchised.

But why should a franchisor allow any unsuitable franchisees through the net? Surely every poor franchisee is a bad reflection on the franchisor? This is quite true, but a franchisor may allow anyone to become a franchisee either through sheer inexperience and lack of knowledge at what makes a good franchisee or as a deliberate ploy if the initial payment of a franchise fee is high enough to make failure profitable for the franchisor.

In such a case we may imagine that a franchisor receives £5,000 as a franchise fee. The training may be poor, and the manual slim and ill-written, with such outlays costing the franchisor no more than 10% of the money he has received. If the franchisee rapidly fails the franchisor can look for a replacement, and in effect sell the same territory at a profit, over and over again.

CHAPTER 2

TOWARDS THE FRANCHISE

Michael Thomas had an idea for a business. He was going to buy in second-hand musical instruments, repair them and then sell them in working order. It sounded to him like a good idea; he enjoyed this type of restoration work and he had done it before and felt he could make money out of it.

Michael first had to check his assumption that he could make money out of the scheme by looking at the following points:

a) He would have to advertise the fact that he was looking for old instruments. How much would each advertisement cost?

b) Each time he advertised, how many people would phone and offer him instruments?

c) Of those instruments offered, how many would be worth buying?

d) How long would it take him to repair each instrument?

e) How much would it cost to repair each instrument?

Michael worked out his answer to each question. Some answers were precise - a classified advertisement in the local paper every night, for example, would cost him £35 per week. But other assumptions were little more than guesses - he thought he would get two instruments offered a night, of which one would be worth buying at the price asked.

Through a series of calculations and guesses of the cost and time involved, Michael concluded that by working all day, and going to see people with instruments for sale in the evening, he could repair five instruments a week. The cost to him would be £35 for the advertisements, £20 a week running costs for his car, £20 a week other expenses and £200 per week personal drawings for him to live on. The total came to £275.

This outlay of £275 would result in five instruments fully repaired and available for sale, which would mean that they would have to be sold, on average, at the price paid plus £55. That seemed a reasonable price to charge and so Michael proceeded although he recognised that many of his calculations were based on little more than guesswork. Would the local newspaper advertisement really result in Michael being able to purchase one instrument a night? Would the amount of work needed to be done on the average instrument be something that he could complete in a single day? Would he really be able to sell the instruments at cost price plus £55 each?

In fact Michael did get some of his estimates wrong, but through perseverance and tenacity he eventually overcame all problems, and turned his idea into a highly successful business which later grew into a sizeable firm, employing half a dozen staff with advertisements placed daily in newspapers throughout ten counties.

Without inside information on the way other people work in the instrument repair trade and the amount of money they make, the questions Michael had to answer at the start could only be answered by inspired guesses. But if Michael had chosen a different route and had decided to buy into a franchise operation then the situation would have been very different. With a franchise all Michael's questions and assumptions would have been answered by the people who set up the original trial run, and further refinements would have been built-in following the experiences of the franchisees. Michael would have taken on far less risk although in the end he would probably have made less money through not being able to expand into other areas, and through having had to pay royalties to the franchisor.

APPROACHING THE FRANCHISOR

Having understood the basic principles of franchising it is now time to start looking around for a suitable franchise to invest in. In choosing a suitable franchise you will probably be guided by the following factors:

YOUR PREVIOUS EMPLOYMENT.

If you have been a salesperson, you may well feel drawn towards any franchise that has a strong personal selling element within it. If you have worked in a print factory, one of the instant print shops may appeal.

YOUR HOBBIES AND INTERESTS.

A strong interest in publishing may direct you towards a local newsletter franchise. Being keen on repairing cars could take you in the direction of a motor trade franchise.

The major areas of work that franchises fall into are shown in the box.

Current areas of franchising in the UK
- Building and household trade (ranging from plumbing to cobblestone paving, re-finishing baths to filling potholes)
- Business services (estate agencies, business transfer, company signs etc)
- Car rental
- Cleaning (house cleaning, factory cleaning, dry cleaning)
- Computers (retail and servicing)
- Fittings and furniture retail
- Food (burgers, pizza, food retail, sandwiches etc)
- Games and physical fitness (adult adventure courses, weight control)
- Gardening (for larger houses and business premises)
- Hair salons
- Interior design (picture framing, blinds, artworks etc)
- Motor trade (car valet, windscreen replacement, clutch replacement, tools etc)
- Photographic (mostly rapid processing)
- Printing ("instant" print services)
- Retail (from supermarkets to carpet shops, cosmetic outlets to ties)
- Transport (mostly overnight courier service)
- Travel agents

THE COST.

Franchises range from investments of under £1000 to over £500,000. Don't overreach yourself. Everyone who starts a business finds it costs more than was planned, and if you borrow to your limit you will have nothing left for emergencies.

WHAT IS AVAILABLE IN YOUR AREA.

If you are not willing to move, you may find that your choice is restricted somewhat.

YOUR WILLINGNESS TO GAMBLE.

Relatively new and untried franchises are much greater risks than tried and tested formulas.

As you consider each of these factors you will want to start approaching franchisors with a view to finding out more. A list of some of the best known franchises is given at the end of this book. If you want to find more you will see that some franchises are regularly advertised in the press. More comprehensive lists of franchises on offer are available in various reference books which you will be able to find in your local reference library. However unless you are using a book which is truly independent and not linked to a franchise magazine or to a consultant, take the comments within them with a pinch of salt. (I must declare my own interest as editor of the GOOD FRANCHISE GUIDE at this point, and leave it to you to decide which publication to use this stage.) The very first approach you are likely to make to any franchise is a request for such basic details as how the franchise works, how much it costs and what it does. Your request might be answered in any one of several ways:

a) It might be ignored. This may sound strange when the franchisor is apparently trying to sell you the franchise package, but research suggests that at least 20% of all requests for franchise information produce no response at all. Some franchisors do not respond to requests for information that come from parts of the country in which they already have franchise operations. (They seem to ignore the possibility of people moving). Others take the view that a lot of the requests they get are from time wasters who write for details from every franchise advertised without any real thought of which ones they might seriously be interested in. Such firms claim that they wait for would-be franchisees to write twice before supplying information. Obviously whether you write a second time depends on how desperate you are for information, but if you do write twice, make sure you state in your letter that this is the second time you have written!

b) Instead of receiving the printed information you have requested you might receive a telephone call or even a personal visit from a representative of the franchisor. The caller may then ask you a lot of questions about your financial position, your background and business experience and so on. If this happens there is always a temptation to give the caller all the information requested, but you should remember that you may be giving away more information than it is in your best interest to do. It is, in my estimation, unreasonable of a franchisor to refuse to give out information to people interested in the business. If you come across such a firm think long and hard about the sort of person you might end up dealing with. If he or she is so bad at communicating from the very start, are you likely to get immediate answers to your questions once you sign up?

c) You might get what you have asked for - details of the franchise.

Such details come in a variety of shapes and sizes - from duplicated sheets to glossy brochures, from simplistic reports full of spelling mistakes and grammatical errors to full colour pictures of head office in the USA.

When you do get these documents, have a quick read through and then consider these questions:

> • Does the brochure tell me exactly how much the franchise is going to cost?

Prices of premises do vary from one part of the country to the other but there ought to be a standard franchise fee mentioned somewhere in the brochure. This is such a basic fact that any franchise brochure which does not answer the question should be treated with caution.

> • Do I know what I will have to buy, lease and rent in order to get started in business?
> • What am I told about training?

Most franchise documents mention training, but some speak vaguely of "our excellent training package specially put together by our team of experts based at headquarters...". What you need is specific information to answer questions such as:

- Is the cost covered in the franchise fee?
- How much practical training is there?
- How much management training is there?
- Is there continuing training once the work has started?
- How many other people are operating this franchise?

Large numbers of people operating a franchise do not guarantee the franchise will be a success for you, but it does give you an indication that you are dealing with an organisation which is up and running rather than just starting. The franchisor should readily supply you with a list of the addresses of the franchisees who are already operational. If not, you may ask yourself why - surely the franchisor is proud of his operations? What has he got to hide?

- How long has the franchisor been in operation?

All businesses have to start sometime, and you may find the franchise that particularly attracts you has only been in operation for a couple of years, but buying into a recently formed franchise has complications. The support may not be as well organised as you might wish, the manual may not be up to standard, and the supply of consumables might not be all that it could be.

- Is the franchise well known to members of the public who might use it?

One of the great advantages of buying into a well-known franchise is the fact that there ought to be willing customers the moment you open. Just how well known is the franchise among its potential customers?
Are you likely to get a response of "I'm glad XYZ Supplies have opened in the town - we've had to travel 30 miles to the nearest shop until now." If so, the omens are positive.

- Is the franchisor a member of any trade associations?

There are no guarantees in this business, and trade association membership may not mean too much but generally it is a positive sign. Membership of the British Franchise Association is well worth noting, although this is not a guarantee of success for there have been a small number of BFA members who have failed, while there are many who are not members of the BFA yet which are highly reputable organisations. However, while being a member of a trade association is not a definitive statement of a company's well-being, generally speaking the more dubious companies are not in such organisations.

> • Is there a full address and phone number I can use for more information?

You would think this is obvious, but astonishingly a number of franchisors do send out material without a phone number and with just a Box number instead of a full address. In either case ask yourself why the franchisor behaves in this way. If you do wish to proceed use the Directory Enquiry service of British Telecom to locate the phone number. If the company is not listed by Directory Enquiries then it is probably nothing more than a private individual operating from home. If you wish to trace a company using a box number telephone the nearest main post office to the address (again Directory Enquiries will supply the number) and ask for the box number office. You are then fully entitled to give the number and have the full postal address read to you - which may suggest whether you are dealing with a proper office or with a private address.

> • How much profit will I make?

All franchises ought to indicate the sort of return you can expect to get on your investment in terms of pre-tax profits in the first three years of trading. They should also show if these figures are calculated before or after drawings or payments made to directors. (If the figures are quoted after franchisee drawings or salary then you will also need to know how much those drawings are).

After considering these initial points some franchises will continue to be of interest to you. Your next action with regard to such companies should be to arrange a visit to an established franchisee.

If you are looking at a franchise which already has 50 or 100 shops dotted around the countryside you can also undertake a brief preliminary review by looking at the shop or factory from the outside, and maybe even going in and making a purchase. However it is not a good idea to declare to the owner of that shop your interest in buying a franchise - a visit with that purpose should be arranged via the franchisor.

If there has been no list of franchisees in the brochure supplied by the franchisor you should ask for one now. But be prepared for disappointment - for some franchisors consistently refuse to give out a list of franchisees. If this happens even after you have declared a positive interest in the franchise you really should be wary - there may be an innocent explanation, but there really might be something to hide.

Explanations given for hiding the names and addresses of franchisees
- It is company policy (The most circular argument of all time)
- We respect their privacy (If you want privacy in business you will probably end up with no customers)
- We don't want them receiving junk mail (If the franchisees are unable to cope with unsolicited letters it does not say much for them)
- We don't want salesmen taking up all their time. (Salesmen make phone calls and turn up in businesses throughout the country. If you don't want to see them you don't have to)

When you visit a franchise on your official visit try to arrange to have a few words in private with the franchisee. If the representative of the franchisor accompanies you on the visit this may not be possible there and then, so ask if the franchisee minds your phoning back later - find a time which will be mutually convenient - and ask any further questions you felt you did not want to ask with the franchisor breathing down your neck.

> **The questions you might consider asking are:**
> • Just how good is the franchisor's support system?
> • Are you making as much money as you expected?
> • Did the training prepare you properly?
> • Is there anything I should be wary of?

After your visit it is time to review the situation to date. Use the following as a check list - if you do not have relevant information on any of these issues go back to the franchisor straight away for more detail. If you feel it is helpful to you to do so, check also with the franchisee whose operation you have visited. You should be able to give an unequivocal "yes" to each of the following:

1. THE FRANCHISE HAS BEEN TRIED AND TESTED
Franchisees should already be out there doing it, and making money doing it. You should be able to find absolute proof of this by visiting premises and talking to people. If the franchise has not been tested, you are not getting one of the main advantages of franchising.

2. ALL NECESSARY MATERIALS ARE SOURCED
If you ever set up in business on your own you will find that locating the various materials and supplies that you need, from reliable suppliers at reasonable prices, takes time. It can also be expensive if items you have ordered and which you need to fulfill customer orders do not turn up. The franchisor should help with this by supplying or putting you in touch with the suppliers of the items you require.

Of course such help can become Draconian if the supplier insists that everything down to the last paper clip is bought through him. Worse, it can become very expensive if the franchisor's prices start rising.

So the issue needs to be looked at both ways - you will probably welcome help in buying materials, but at a reasonable price.

3. THE FRANCHISOR CAN SUPPLY CONSTANT SUPPORT AND GUIDANCE
We have already mentioned that there needs to be initial training. But there needs to be something else as well - constant support once you have started - especially in the early weeks of the franchise. In your judgement, is it likely that you will be able to pick up the phone and ask even the most

mundane question and get a clear and immediate answer?   Did the franchisor you spoke with confirm this to be so?

4. THERE SHOULD BE HELP WITH ACCOUNTS, VAT etc

One of the major problems that many franchisees face is that of keeping accounts, making VAT and tax returns, keeping staff payment records and the like. All franchisors ought to offer a wide range of help on this to ensure that you get your figures right in a minimum amount of time, leaving you free to concentrate on production and selling.

5. GOVERNMENT REGULATIONS

Many aspects of business are controlled by government and local authority regulations which can cover everything from employment agencies to food shops. Finding out which regulations you have to obey, which department in local or national government to deal with and what forms to fill in can take a massive amount of time. All this should be short circuited by the franchisor who should know where to go and what to do.

6. BANK HELP

Raising money is something most of us to have to do when we open a business. When approached by a person going into business on their own for the first time, banks are often cautious and may lend you far less than you want. With a franchise the banks normally lend more readily. All the leading banks have their own franchise division, and if a reference to that division with your request for money does not result in the money being forthcoming you should ask why. If the bank is unhappy with the financial prospects of the franchise that is something you should be aware of.

7. ADVERTISING AND PUBLICITY

Finding out which advertising works and which does not can be a very expensive business. Most advertising - be it direct mail or display advertising in trade or consumer magazines - will cost hundreds of pounds a time, and it is easy to assume that a particular advertisement will bring in trade only to find that it does not.

Worse still, in many cases it is difficult to see just how successful an advertisement has been. You may get an upturn in trade after an advertisement appears but you might have got that anyway without the advertisement. Only with months or years of testing can you really find out how successful or otherwise your advertising is. The franchisor should have very clear information based on research which you can inspect to help you consider suitable ways to promote the business, and the franchisor should also help arrange the launch promotion.

8. STOCK CONTROL, SALES CONTROL, CREDIT CONTROL

At all times it is important to know exactly where your business is and where it is going. If you run out of vital goods just when your customers need them, if you are owed so much money by customers that you have no money left to pay your suppliers, if goods you have ordered do not turn up on time, then your business can fail. In each case this failure will not be because the business itself is no good, but simply because you are not handling the basic administration of the business correctly. The franchisor will not run the business for you, but should certainly help you set up a proven system that will ensure that you do not go into liquidation.

9. THE PRODUCT OR SERVICE SHOULD BE OF PROVEN VALUE AND SHOULD BE IMPROVING ALL THE TIME

Part of the franchisor's responsibility is to deliver to you a package which works now and will work for the foreseeable future. This means a product or service that is changing with the changing market place.

We live in a dynamic world, and all business operations need constant development if they are to maintain their position, and indeed grow. Research and development costs money, and the franchisor should be paying for this. This research should be generating results - ask existing franchisees what new ideas have been implemented since they started, and if they have been successful.

10. THERE SHOULD BE HELP WITH SELECTION OF SITES

Some franchises actually obtain a suitable site for you, but even if they do not, every help should be given with selecting a site, obtaining planning permission, clearing building regulations and negotiating a suitable lease. The franchise contract should not come into operation unless and until a viable site is found and agreed upon. Your deposit should be returned at once if it proves impossible to locate a suitable site.

11. GUIDANCE SHOULD BE GIVEN
IN SELECTING INITIAL STOCK LEVELS

It is very easy to buy-in too little (and keep customers waiting) or too much (and tie up too much capital). It is equally easy to buy-in the wrong lines. The franchisor's experience should enable you to avoid all these expensive mistakes.

12. LEGAL HELP AND PROTECTION

None of us imagines that we will need legal help when we start in business, but many companies do find situations arise in which they need some guidance, if not actual help in court. The franchisor should be aware of all the tricks and slips that can lead to legal arguments, and should be able to help you avoid them. Find out if legal help is centralised and free. The centralisation of legal advice through one firm specialising in the franchise's concerns can be very helpful if similar types of problem turn up again and again.

A CHECK-LIST OF THE ADVANTAGES OF TAKING UP A FRANCHISE

- The business format is already established
- Established sources for products
- Training before you begin, and support once you have started
- Clear guidance with advertising and publicity
- Help with accounts, finance, legal questions and administration
- Help in choosing a site, negotiating a lease and setting stock levels
- Constant research and development by the franchisor to improve the product or service all the time.

If you can't see all these advantages take care, and ask yourself why such fundamental advantages of franchising should be missing from the franchise you are considering.

CHAPTER 3

IS FRANCHISING RIGHT FOR ME?

Having started to consider the advantages of taking up a franchise, you should now spend some time evaluating yourself - are you the right person to become a successful franchisee?

Let us start by considering whether or not you are going to benefit from one of the main advantages of franchising - help with administration.

Imagine this situation: You are the owner of a new business selling double-edged sprocket loaders to the building trade. You have two staff who take phone calls and deal with builders and DIY fanatics as they beat a path to your door seeking out your product. The first month has been hard work but worthwhile, and you feel you are on to something.

For most of the time you have been so busy actually making the double-edged sprocket loaders that you have not had time to catch up on the messages and notes that your assistants have been placing on your desk.

Now they are hovering outside your office waiting to be paid, and you remember that throughout the past month you have been putting off reading that 250-page manual that the Inland Revenue sent you on deducting tax from your staff's payroll. Then there is the equally massive tome from the Department of Health and Social Security on making

National Insurance deductions from pay. You have no idea how to calculate how much money to deduct.

Your eye strays to the note pad. With mounting horror you read that Smudget and Co will be closed for the next two weeks for annual leave and will not be able to supply any side brackets for your widgets. All pre-vacation orders should have been placed by yesterday. You know you are going to run out in two days time.

Another note says that Loggit and Loggit from whom you bought your opening stock of steel have phoned to say that if within three days payment does not arrive for the steel supplied two months ago when you began making sprockets, legal action will follow without further notice. As you wonder where you put their invoice you see another note stating that Philpotts have phoned asking if their order of 3000 units can be supplied on Monday rather than Thursday...

And so it goes on. It is not too much of an exaggeration to state that if you have never actually run a business you cannot imagine the amount of organisational activity that goes on day by day. With a business that has been running a few years it all looks so simple - somehow the administration gets done without it being noticeable. Everyone knows what to do. What is easy to forget with such a business is that there will have been a long learning process to get to the stage where day-to-day administration progresses that easily.

To evaluate how much you need the sort of help and guidance a good franchise can give you, think how you would solve each of the above problems.

If you have a wealth of experience in running a business then such tales as that of our double-edged sprocket loader producer will not worry you in the slightest. But for someone who in the past has always been an employee the whole thing takes on the air of learning to drive a car. Everyone else does it so you think it must be easy.

As you first try and let out the clutch and push down the accelerator (remembering to watch the rear view mirror and ensure you are actually in first rather than reverse) you begin your struggle with the controls and wonder how anyone has ever got the hang of such an operation. Once you have driven for a few years you may find it hard to imagine how anyone can find driving at all difficult.

So it is with business. If you have experience of working out PAYE, stock control, credit control, management accounts and the like, then one of the great advantages of being a franchisee will not apply to you; you will already know how to do it. If you lack that experience it is still possible to go it alone, but franchising would make life a lot easier and enable you to make a profit in much less time.

Being a franchisee will remove some of the pressures that every newcomer to business feels, but you should not believe that signing on the dotted line as a franchisee will mean you don't have to learn about management accounts, PAYE and the like. You will still have to fill in the tax and National Insurance forms, you will still have to deal with other businesses who owe you money, and you will still have to ensure your bought ledger is under control. To help, you will have pre-launch training and day-to-day guidance once you get going.

However if the mere thought of paperwork and administration sends you back into the workshop in a cold sweat then franchising will not help you, for as the managing director of your firm you will still have to ensure that administration takes place. The franchisor will give guidance but will not undertake the basic day-to-day activities that are part of any business.

One solution that does occur to some highly practical men and women is to suggest that their other halves will undertake the paperwork. "We will work as a team," is the phrase one often hears in these circumstances. This is fine as long as the spouse appreciates what is lined up, and if he or she too takes part in the training sessions or has a background in administration. But what will not work is for the franchisee to attend sessions on book keeping, not understand a word, excuse himself/herself on the grounds that "my wife/husband will do that" and then find that although highly willing the spouse really has no idea how to handle taxation and accountancy. If you are planning to work as a team, enquire if it is possible to register as joint franchisees, and ensure that both of you go on the training sessions.

Becoming the proud owner of a business has more to do with working seven days a week and not stopping until midnight than sitting in a swivel chair behind a large desk complete with leather inlay and dictating orders over the internal phone. Working into the nights and at weekends are not just occasional extras when the business is busy. The vast majority of successful self-employed people state that for the first three years such behaviour is the norm. Indeed in a recent survey of franchisees carried out by the GOOD FRANCHISE GUIDE the one comment that franchisees made over and over again was, "it is such hard work". In other words being a franchisee is not a way of avoiding the hard work of self-employment. Indeed it can be the opposite as the franchisor insists that high standards and full scale operations are maintained.

But it will not just be you, the franchisee who is affected. As a franchisee moves from being employed to being self-employed, the change in working conditions will have a major impact on his or her whole family. It is not unknown for the change-over to be one that creates a great deal of pride in a family, - one's own business, headed paper showing the franchisee's name as managing director, the spouse as company secretary - the first customers, the first cheques - it all seems very exciting.

As time goes by strains begin to tell. To see how you will react answer the following questions:

1. What do you normally do at weekends? Do you take the children out, go shopping, drive to the countryside or beach, undertake DIY repairs in the house...?

2. What do you normally do in the evenings?

3. How many holidays do you take a year? Bank holidays, two weeks at Christmas, two weeks in the summer? Occasional days?

4. How many days off have you had during the past three years for illness?

Now imagine that because of pressure of work you work every Saturday and most Sundays. You also work most evenings, through the Christmas break, and through the summer. No matter how ill you feel you still have to go into work. How will the rest of your family feel about that?

Most franchisees who are successful in overcoming such problems do so through having very full discussions within the family about the difficulties before the business gets under way. After all, if everyone recognises that you will have three years of very hard work, but then will reap the benefits later, those three years become much more bearable.

Speaking of the family, if you as franchisee have the expectation that one or more members of your family will work with you it is vital that the exact nature of this help is spelled out and agreed long before the franchise agreement is signed.

The worse that can happen is that a vague promise that "I'll be happy to help out" is given by your spouse. Help out doing what? When? Where? One half of the family might assume this means working in the shop every day serving customers while the other half sees it as popping down to the bank with the cash and cheques or covering for the odd half day once a month. If husband and wife are both to be working then many other questions arise:

- who will look after the children, especially during the holidays?
- who will shop for the food and cook the meals?
- who will be the arbiter when differences of opinion arise on the conduct of the business?
- can both husband and wife get on well seeing each other not only at home but at work as well?

Of course millions of families do survive with both husband and wife going out to work every day. And tens of thousands of families have husband and wife working together. But if you have not tried these arrangements before, think them through carefully first.

Remember, you already fill up your days with activities, and many of these activities will have to stop once you start working for yourself. Do you mind?

DEALING WITH PEOPLE

Running your own business is not only about your own hard work, it is also about being able to get others to work hard. Getting the right people to work for you (indeed in some parts of the country getting anyone to work for you) is hard enough. Getting them to work hard is a totally different matter.

For the new franchisee matters are made even more complicated than for someone who has set up his or her own business. Firstly as a new franchisee you are new to the job which means you have not got years of experience in solving each and every problem. You don't know what mistakes can be made, and you don't have the experience to look for them in advance. Of course this is true for every self-employed person, but the difference for the person starting alone from scratch is that he or she will be able to start slowly. It is not unknown for businesses to start in a spare bedroom, building to a turnover of £500,000 within four or five years. Yet in the early months the owner of this business was able to learn the ins and outs of trading on a turnover of perhaps just £1000 per month. No franchisor will ever allow a franchisee to start at home, unless the whole business is based around the idea of working from home.

Secondly, as your business starts up you will be incredibly busy, too busy in fact to train and supervise each new member of staff properly.

Put these two factors together and it is vital that you have an ability to recruit the right people and use them in the best way possible.

At the same time as handling your own staff you have to be able to handle your customers. "The customer is always right" is a phrase we all know, but when you find yourself being taken for a ride by a customer who you know is absolutely in the wrong (but you can't prove it without disrupting a lot of your work) then you will need all your people-handling skills to keep your business and yourself on an even keel.

You have to want to deal with people and be able to deal with people to be any good in running a franchise. You will know what you feel like and what you enjoy. And if you have never had any experience with staff take every opportunity to watch others do it.

So far we have dealt with the various characteristics you have to have in order to be a success in a franchise. You need to be able to work hard, have the support of family, and be able to handle both paper work and people. All these characteristics relate equally well to setting up in virtually any business on your own, although as we have seen the franchisee is forced to start at full strength. But is there any attribute which is special to the successful franchisee, but which does not apply to people setting up entirely on their own?

The answer is yes - a willingness to fit into a system. The whole point of a franchise is that the format of the business already exists, and the aim is for the franchisee to apply it to his or her territory. That means you need to be able to listen to and read what others say about the system, and while not accepting their words as gospel, take what is said as correct until proved otherwise.

For the business starting up without a franchise, a different set of criteria applies. Here, in order to succeed, the would-be entrepreneur needs to analyse everything, question everything and have a solid streak of practical creativity which can be applied to the task in hand. The newly self-employed person needs to be full of bright ideas and have the ability to perceive in advance and then reject the concepts which will not work.

Of course the franchisee needs to be creative at times in adapting the franchise format to local situations, but a franchisee who buys into a pizza restaurant franchise and in his first week comes up with the bright idea that if the table cloths were yellow instead of red profit would be doubled should probably not be a franchisee at all.

This is not to say that the franchisee cannot have creative ideas, but rather he or she should realise from the start that fitting into the system comes before refining it.

The franchisee works in a curious world which combines being the Managing Director of a business in charge of a team of employees with running the operation along the lines laid down by the franchisor. If the amount of control the franchisor might have over you worries you, and if you are concerned at how your creative sparkle might be dampened, then take a good look at the contract, and talk to other franchisees already working this franchise. Remember once you have paid your franchise fee it is hard to get it back.

CHECK-LIST FOR
WOULD BE FRANCHISEES

- Can you cope with book keeping?
- Are you willing to give up most of your spare time for the next three years including public holidays, evenings and weekends?
- Is your family willing to put up with not seeing much of you for the next three years?
- If you are planning to involve any of your family in the business, are you and they both fully aware and in full agreement as to what they are going to do?
- Do you like dealing with people, and are you good at getting the best out of people?
- When you see a business do you immediately think how you could fit in with that system, or do you immediately think of ways that it could be improved.

CHAPTER 4

VARIATIONS ON THE FRANCHISING THEME

Once you start looking for franchises that may interest you, you are bound to come across business opportunities which may have elements in common with franchising but which are not franchises in the full sense of the word. These range from the very attractive add-on franchise which exists as a full franchise but has the additional criteria that the operation is added on to an existing business, to schemes which border on the illegal. Sadly some of these dubious schemes serve to give all types of franchising a bad name which is certainly not deserved. Some common schemes are described below.

THE DISTRIBUTORSHIP

A recognised distributor agrees to hold a certain amount of stock from Company X, in return for a particular level of discount on each item bought in for re-sale. A typical example is Jon's Garages which sell new and secondhand Volvo cars. Jon agrees to have not less than five new

Volvos in his showroom at any one time and to carry certain spare parts for cars that are serviced. In return Volvo Concessionaires (who import Volvo from Sweden) agree to give Jon a specific discount from the list price on each car. In addition Volvo agree not to let any other garage within 25 miles in any direction have a Volvo distributorship agreement.

ADVANTAGE:

If the product or service is well-known and well liked customers will automatically seek you out. Make your showroom or shop more attractive than your rivals and you can increase your share of the market.

DISADVANTAGE:

You are tied to one product, and if its desirability in the eyes of the public falls there is nothing you can do about it. You are totally in the hands of head office.

THE LICENSEE

The licensee has permission to produce certain goods or use a trade name, a person's name or a logo. For example, Jack Fairweather invents a remarkable new photocopying process. He patents the system and then allows others to build photocopy machines using his process under licence. Meanwhile Jack's brother David has just signed for Arsenal Football Club and become the league's top goal scorer. He agrees a deal with Sockaboot, the manufacturers of a particular style of football boots through which the style of boot will be re-named Fairweather Boots, with David's face appearing in advertisements for the boots. Both Jack and David are offering licences, one for an invention and one for a famous name.

ADVANTAGE:

In becoming a licensee you gain access to something of proven worth for a fixed sum of money; this means you can calculate your costs exactly in advance.

DISADVANTAGE:

You may have committed your money to a licence only to find that someone else invents a better product six months later.

THE ADD-ON FRANCHISE

Add-on franchises can be of great interest to anyone who is currently running their own business, and feels they would like to expand through developing an additional area of work. This area of work may be directly related to the work already undertaken - as when a garage that repairs and sells cars decides to add on a car rental franchise.

An add-on franchise can alternatively be unrelated as when a manufacturing business becomes a depot for an overnight courier service.

ADVANTAGE:

The great advantage to the franchisor of the add-on franchise is that it is easier to distinguish the ability of any potential franchisee if one can ask questions about his or her existing business. The franchisor will be able to judge very quickly if the franchisee knows about invoicing, accounts, taxation, ordering, record keeping and so on by looking at the state of the records in the existing business.

For the franchisee the great advantage normally is that he already has premises. It is also possible that some staff can be shared between the new franchised business and the existing business, and it is even possible for phone lines to be shared. All this cuts out a lot of time and expense in locating premises, kitting out an office and the many other costs involved in setting up a new business.

While the number of add-on franchises on the market is small, it is not impossible for franchises which are primarily intended as separate businesses to be added to existing companies. Obviously the franchisor's permission must be given for this, and where a distinctive shop front in a certain sector of town is required such permission may be withheld, but in other businesses which are not dependent upon a high street presence, spare space can often be utilised by setting up a separate franchise. Indeed it is not unknown for people with their own premises to put in a mezzanine floor, or to fit out another part of their office and warehouse space to develop in this way.

DISADVANTAGE:

None unless the add-on franchise takes up more space, time or finance than you originally considered.

MULTI-LEVEL MARKETING
AND PYRAMID SELLING

From the sublime to the ridiculous we move from the highly attractive world of the add-on franchise to the highly dubious world of multi- level marketing.

Because of the success of much franchising, the high profile of some of the best known franchises, and the widely accepted fact that firms are less likely to go out of business if they are franchised, many businesses which are not franchises try to use the word "franchise" as part of their description of themselves. This is particularly so where the "franchisee" finds himself closely related to the business promoter and dependent upon him for the work.

Obviously each case must be taken on its merits, but two particular types of scheme should be mentioned here because they sound most beguiling and yet verge on the illegal. They are traditionally known as pyramid selling schemes, or more recently multi-level marketing schemes (although it must be admitted there are some multi-level schemes which are legitimate and not related to pyramid schemes).

In the typical scheme, the "franchisee" buys in a quantity of the product that is to be sold, and then has the option of selling it to the general public or to another distributor or "franchisee". It does not take long to realise that the goods are difficult to sell to the public, often because they are hopelessly overpriced, and that the best way to make money is through setting up other people as distributors to whom you can sell your goods. These distributors, in turn then sell on to yet more distributors! The product becomes irrelevant save as a symbol of being a distributor.

Contrary to popular belief pyramid schemes are not illegal in themselves. However the Fair Trading Act does require that anyone joining the scheme should be able to withdraw without penalty within one week of signing up. It also stipulates that no claim should be made that a particular income will be earned. Further, in relation to the goods themselves there should be a limit on the price 'franchisees' have to pay (to stop the pyramid going on for ever with higher and higher prices) and the originator of the scheme has to be willing to buy back all the stock held at 90% of the price paid if someone wishes to pull out of the scheme.

The simplest way to spot such a scheme is to ask yourself if a) you are being forced to buy in a lot of stock in advance, and b) if you will make more money finding new dealers rather than selling stock to the general public.

One variation of this theme has come with operations in which the goods that are sold are very simple to reproduce - for example photocopied sheets of information. The goods are sold on and on continuously, but no-one makes any money out of the information provided save by selling it on to the next person.

Of course the overwhelming majority of franchisors have nothing to do with this sort of selling, but it is worth noting that some franchises do require the franchisee to buy in a certain level of stock before trading begins. In such cases you should always ask yourself if you will be able to re-sell your stock to the supplier at 90% of its cost to you. It is not an unreasonable request to make in the event of something going wrong, especially as you are paying a franchise fee for the privilege of selling the goods in the first place.

ADVANTAGE:
None, unless you like flirting with the law and deliberately defrauding people.

DISADVANTAGE:
The schemes normally only work for those people who originate them; the people whom you defraud might wish to take revenge, and you may receive an unpleasant letter from the Department of Trade and Industry.

AN OVERSEAS FRANCHISE

Returning from the unsavoury world of pyramid selling we come to the perfectly legitimate world of the overseas franchise. Many franchises that start in another country set up a master franchise in the UK through which normal area franchises are available. If you find a franchise which originally comes from overseas, but is by now well established in the UK you will have no need to consider the company in any way differently from the way you would consider a British franchise.

However, you may find an overseas franchisor operating with little more than a simple office in the UK, selling the franchise on the basis of its high success in America or elsewhere. Such a company may be attempting to finance itself by selling its first two or three franchises without having set up its support structure first or even having run a UK pilot scheme.

There certainly is an attractiveness about being in on the ground floor with a new development which has been proven to work elsewhere.

However, you should remember that not every idea can be transferred from one country to another, and many that can be transferred can only be transferred with great modification to the style of promotion and sometimes even to the product itself. You should therefore think carefully about any foreign franchise which is not already well established in the UK, and be wary about believing that high profits from one country can automatically be realised in another.

ADVANTAGE:

The oversees operator may have spotted a hole in the UK market which can be exploited using a combination of British know-how and experience gained in the overseas operation.

DISADVANTAGE:

If the scheme sinks without trace there is little likelihood of support from franchisees spread world-wide. Also, watch out for problems that can arise if the manual has been imported from the USA without a total re-write. Business in America is totally different from business in the UK, and an American manual may prove to be totally inadequate for your needs.

BUYING OUT AN EXISTING FRANCHISEE

As an alternative to setting up as a franchisee from scratch you may wish to buy out an existing franchisee. People may wish to sell existing franchise outlets for any number of reasons - and you should try an identify which reasons apply in any case you consider. Remember, the person selling the franchise may tell you truthfully why he or she is selling, or may alternatively try to hide the truth in order to effect a sale. You have to play detective. Here are a number of explanations you might be given.

EXPLANATION:

Have done it for several years, done fairly well but have had enough of the hard work.

Comments:

Franchises are hard work, and there is nothing wrong in wanting to find something easier, nor in seeking a change after a number of years.

EXPLANATION:
Have been making a very good profit and want to capitalise on that.

Comments:
Here you will have to pay a heavy premium to buy into a proven winner. Look out for any signs that the situation in the franchise may be about to change (new franchisor, local changes etc) and for suggestions that the success has been down to the sheer genius of the franchisee. If local people buy from that franchise outlet because of the current owner sales will slip when he or she sells out no matter what you do.

EXPLANATION:
Have had a sudden change in personal circumstances.

Comments:
This can happen to all of us, the personal circumstances in question ranging from a divorce of the husband and wife who run the operation to a sudden windfall from the death of a long-lost relative in South America. Difficult to check on someone else's personal history, but look out and see if there might be any other reasons.

EXPLANATION:
Have done fairly well, but can see disasters round the corner and are getting out before its too late.

Comments:
The story given will probably be different - personal circumstances change, need a change of scene or whatever. If there are any changes on the horizon, either locally or nationally, which the vendors do not willingly disclose then take the coincidence of wanting to sell up for another reason with caution.

EXPLANATION:
Have done fairly well, but just can't stand the sight of the franchisor.

Comments:
Ask the franchisor for an opinion of the franchisee. Check with other franchisees for their opinion of the franchisor.

EXPLANATION:
Have been making a loss.

Comments:

And what makes you think you can do better? Of course it is possible that you are God's gift to selling, and you will rapidly turn a loss- making operation around. But remember, if part of the problem is the bad image that the franchise has generated in its own locality then the expedient of an 'Under new management' sign may not achieve too much.

WORKING FROM HOME

Working from home is not so much a variety on franchising but rather an approach adopted by certain franchisees with the permission or even encouragement of the franchisor, the main advantage being that premises do not have to be sought, and there should be a considerable saving on rent. In a case such as this a few words of guidance, if not warning may be in order.

Planning permission. Houses and flats are meant to be lived in not used as business premises. In recent years local authorities have taken an increasingly relaxed view of people working at home, in line with the government's attempts to encourage the development of small businesses. However in many cases this still represents little more than turning a blind eye to the relevant regulations, and problems may arise if you have neighbours who are given grounds for complaint.

Certainly, if you sit at home making and taking phone calls, employing at most one or two other people to do the filing then it is unlikely that anyone will know that you are in business. If however you start a car repair business in your garage and leave engines scattered around your drive while customers come and go throughout the day and evening, you could be asking for trouble.

No hard and fast rules exist, and certainly if you don't employ anyone you are unlikely to need any form of permission to work from home unless your customers make a nuisance of themselves.

ADVANTAGE:

As already stated you overcome the problem of finding and paying for business premises. What is more if things do go wrong in the business you will have one major commitment less than would otherwise be the case.

DISADVANTAGE:

If the local authority does take an interest in what you are doing at home you could find yourself forced to apply for planning permission for a change of use of the house, and then after waiting some time, have it refused! Watch out also for problems with the Inland Revenue who may claim that part of the profit you make when you sell your house is actually taxable since part of your house was used for business. Try to avoid using one room exclusively for business purposes, and be restrained in the amount of your lighting and heating bills that you claim against tax.

HANDS UP THOSE WHO DIDN'T TALK TO US.

Even with the best will in the world, a poorly planned franchising project will never get off the ground.

That's why, whether you're thinking of franchising or becoming a franchisee yourself, we recommend you talk to The Royal Bank of Scotland first.

With many years in this field alone, we've developed a keen sense for a sound proposition.

We know the best ways to approach and execute a plan, as well as being able to provide any necessary financial muscle.

And once we've taken you under our wing, we'll continue to support and advise you with any future expansion ideas.

So if you think your venture has legs, contact our Franchise Managers at Head Office or at our London or Manchester addresses.

The Royal Bank of Scotland
WHERE PEOPLE MATTER

Registered Office: 36 St Andrew Square, Edinburgh EH2 2YB. Registered in Scotland No. 90312.
The Royal Bank of Scotland plc. Head Office, 42 St Andrew Square, Edinburgh EH2 2YE. Tel: 031-556 8555.
The Royal Bank of Scotland plc. Regent's House, PO Box 348, 42 Islington High Street, London N1 8XL. Tel: 01-833 2121.
The Royal Bank of Scotland plc, Centurion House, 129 Deansgate, Manchester M3 3WR. Tel: 061-236 8585.

CHAPTER 5

SOURCES OF FINANCE

As you begin to consider which franchises might be of interest to you, you will need to look at how much money you have got to invest, and how much you might be able to borrow. Following that is the question, "Who should I try and borrow the money from?"

> **The most common sources of finance for franchisees are:**
> a) own savings
> b) redundancy money
> c) money borrowed from parents and friends
> d) money from the bank

Before you talk to any outside agency about funding you should draw up a business plan which shows all of the following factors:

a) Details of yourself.

This should be a very brief summary of what you have done previously in so far as it is related to the franchise you now plan to take up.

What you do not need to describe is each job you have had in turn - the briefest summary will do. Only give fuller details where there is relevance to what you now propose, either because the franchise is in the same field as the job, or because the work you undertook gave you financial or other essential experience.

b) The business idea.

Describe the business - what is produced, what service is offered, what is sold, the type of customer.

c) The franchisor.

How many franchisees exist already, details of the franchisor's finances and past record of success.

d) How much is needed and what for.

List of all the money that is needed, what it is needed for, give a cashflow forecast and related financial information.

As you will see, most of the information that you are required to give should be available from the franchisor, and will merely need you to put it together in a suitable format that will impress upon any financial institution you approach that this is a serious application.

The first person that you should talk to should be your bank manager, for even if you do not borrow all the money you need from him, you will almost certainly need to utilise overdraft and other facilities in due course. What is more, at this stage in the proceedings a bank manager is a source of free professional advice, which is always worth having.

It will be very difficult for the manager to give you clear and fair responses to your propositions and questions unless he knows exactly what you are planning, how much money you need, what your commitments are likely to be, and what assets you have to back up your financial requirements.

Making things look better than they really are when talking to any financial adviser is silly and invariably leads to trouble. Tell the bank the truth at all times. You should remember that most people tell their bank managers nothing until they are in trouble. The sophisticated borrower on the other hand goes in the opposite direction and tells the manager everything he might need to know and more. If you are planning to use your house as a guarantee of your borrowing, invite your bank manager out to see your house. If you have a factory or shop site in mind, invite him along to look at it. And if you think you will probably need to borrow £25,000, tell your bank manager you expect the sum to be £30,000. Then, if you are wrong and more is needed you do not have to make an admission of having made an error. On the other hand if your initial projection turns out to have been correct you can gain credit for having dealt judiciously with suppliers and set your business up for less than planned.

It is at this point that your bank manager can be particularly helpful in the advice given. If the bank refuses to lend you the money you feel you will need, the manager will usually give reasons why, and those reasons should be considered at length. All the major clearing banks now have franchising divisions, and they are constantly in the business of looking for new customers. They will therefore not send you away empty-handed if they think that there is a strong chance of your making a success of your venture. What is more, banks are generally keen on franchises because most recognised and well- established franchises result in profits for the franchisees. But if despite this the bank does not want to know, you really must find out why.

If the bank with which you have worked for some time does not want to support you, and if you feel that their reasons for this lack of support are inappropriate, you will have to start looking elsewhere for finance. Having been turned down by one bank does not preclude you from approaching the other clearing banks, and it is quite common for a proposition which is unacceptable to one bank to be approved by another. What may happen to you is that the bank may offer to meet part of your requirements through an overdraft facility and a business development loan, while suggesting an alternative scheme for raising the rest of the finance you require. The various alternatives are described below. Firstly the two most common, and normally the cheapest, ways of borrowing money. The first - the overdraft, offers a way of securing short-term finance, the second - the business development loan - supplies finance for longer term borrowings.

OVERDRAFT.

The overdraft is the prime way of keeping a business afloat with regards its short-term requirements. The bank allows its customer to write cheques which take the account into deficit up to an agreed point, on the understanding that these cheques are for current requirements only, not for the purchasing of fixed assets.

BUSINESS DEVELOPMENT LOANS.

These are loans which are for a specified sum required for a particular purpose (e.g. 6000 install lighting and heating in a factory, lay carpets, and so on.) The money is repaid monthly over a set period (often two, three or five years) along with interest, which can either be at a pre-determined rate, or a variable rate. Which you choose depends on how much you like gambling and what other commitments you have. Certainly the fixed rate of interest does mean that you can plan your finances much more easily.

Having looked at the most common ways of borrowing money we can now consider the alternatives which may be used when the prime sources fail to provide enough finance.

ALTERNATIVE SOURCES FOR LONG-TERM BORROWINGS

LOAN GUARANTEES

If your bank feels that the loan you require is a viable one, but for some reason the bank does not wish to loan you the money, the bank can approve the application and pass it on to the Department of Trade and Industry (DTI) with a request for a loan guarantee. If accepted by the DTI, the loan is repaid at a rate above the normal rates quoted by the banks, over a period of up to seven years. The loan is guaranteed in the sense that if you fail to make your re-payments part of the loan is guaranteed by the DTI so the bank does not lose out. Certain types of business are excluded from the scheme - the main ones which affect franchising being estate agencies, pubs and insurance companies.

Loan guarantee schemes are worth looking at if you really are unable to raise the money in any other way, and if the return on your money is likely to be so good that the extra interest is of no concern to you.

LEASING

It is possible to lease cars, photocopiers, franking machines, and a wide range of other types of items of equipment. Under a lease arrangement you (the lessee) do not own the equipment but have full use of it in return for paying a monthly sum to the owner (the lessor). There is also normally tied into the agreement a maintenance deal. Most typically a photocopier may be obtained on a monthly lease of say £50.00, plus a charge of 1.5p per copy made. The £50.00, which is fixed and cannot be varied at all, is to be paid for five years, at the end of which the payment is reduced to £50 per year. Even at this stage you do not own the photocopier, but you are leasing it at a much lower rate since by now it is five years old and clearly very out of date. The 1.5p per copy however can vary, and inflation may increase this as time goes by. This sum is related to maintenance, and gives you the right to call out an engineer free of charge whenever the machine goes wrong. (There will always be other technicalities - you may have to pay for replacement parts when worn out, and you will certainly have to pay for consumables such as paper and toner.)

Leasing has the advantage that it does not tie up your capital. If you keep an item for a long time the real cost of the lease will decline as inflation takes other prices up (the converse is true in a deflationary environment). If you want to get rid of the item you will find that someone is willing to buy the lease in as part of the deal of fixing you up with a new machine.

The disadvantage of leasing is that closing a lease before the end of its term is expensive - especially if not taken as part of a new deal to lease another item. What is more, the actual cost of having an item on lease can be very high indeed - and paying over the top for a lease is a risk you run if you use a leasing company nominated by the franchisor, or by the firm trying to persuade you to take a particular product. If you are to take on a lease always get prices from two or three leasing companies to compare with the one you are quoted by the franchisor or the salesman. (One way to check if a salesman is getting a commission on a lease - which will of course be paid for by you - is to ask what the price for the photocopier or whatever would be if you paid cash. If the salesman cannot give you an immediate answer then the chances are that a commission is being paid on the lease and you are being asked to pay too much for the lease.)

HIRE PURCHASE

This is a variant on leasing which leaves you the owner of the product after you have made the payments (but not until every payment has been completed). HP is an expensive way of buying and should only be considered when other forms of purchase have proven to be unavailable to you, although prices can vary especially if the manufacturer or retail outlet is stimulating sales through discounting the cost of the HP agreement. However you should be aware that you cannot sell an item for which the HP payments have not all been made since you clearly cannot sell something you do not own. (Some people do sell items bought on HP and use the money received to pay off the remaining payments, but this is contrary to all HP agreements, and you should ensure that you do not buy anything which is already subject to an HP agreement.)

MORTGAGES

Mortgages are loans which allow a person or company to buy property. The property itself is nominally owned by the purchaser from the start, but if he or she defaults on repayments then the lender can take over the building and sell it in order to reclaim the cost of the loan.

Buying a property will always cost more over the 10 year period of purchase than renting the same building, although you will get some tax relief (providing you are making a profit!). Owning the property will help make your balance sheet look good, but that value is then totally locked up in the building and cannot easily be used. The biggest gamble you are taking on the building is that when you wish to sell it, the hope is that it has increased in value. If it has, you can make a major profit. But if you come to sell in a recession you may find yourself with an unsaleable asset on your hands. What is more, if you are selling in order to move into another property the chances are that all your profit will immediately be eaten up by the cost of the next building.

Perhaps the best advice to be given is that buying a property can be seen as an investment (although risky), and if after taking on your franchise you expect to have sufficient spare funds to be able to do this and you fancy a gamble on a large scale, you can consider buying.

ALTERNATIVES FOR SHORT-TERM FINANCE

FACTORING

If your business sells directly to the public you will get cash (or its immediate equivalent through cheques and credit card payments) each time you sell an item. However if you sell to other businesses then much, if not all that you sell, will be on credit. It is quite possible that a company with a turnover of £100,000 will be owed £10,000 at any one time, and a company with a turnover of £500,000 might be owed £40,000. Such sums would be very useful to the company if only they could get their hands on them quickly, rather than having to wait for the money to be paid by the debtors.

Factoring agencies allow you to get your hands on this money rapidly. The agency pays part of the money to you as soon as the invoice is issued, (normally around 80%) and then endeavour to collect the money in from the debtor. Some such agencies may provide a full service of debt chasing and collecting, but experience shows that others simply send out computerised reminders and computerised threats about court action, which are largely ignored by the debtors (who can of course recognise a factor's computer when they see one). What this means is that some three months after the invoice was issued payment may not yet have been collected by the factoring agency who merely hand the invoice back, and take back all the money originally paid out on that invoice. This can be a disaster of course since by then the invoice can be three months old, which can make it a difficult bill to collect.

All in all there can be disadvantages in factoring and normally you should only consider it when other forms of finance are not available.

CREDIT CONTROL

Effective credit control means getting those people who owe you money to pay you quickly. The faster they pay you the more money there is in your account, and the less you need to raise money from elsewhere.

Quite how you get money in rapidly varies from business to business - it depends on who your customers are, and how polite you need to be to avoid causing them to take their work elsewhere.

The largest area where effective credit control can have an impact is in relation to your dealings with small or medium companies that buy from you only once or twice a year. In such cases timely reminders of overdue accounts can work wonders. To increase the likelihood of your money being received rapidly you should bear the following rules in mind:

1. When sending out a reminder always send a copy invoice (clearly marked "copy"). This stops the traditional game of "please send a copy we have lost the original."
2. Don't make threats you are not equipped to carry out. Don't threaten court action unless you know how to do it, or have a solicitor waiting to pounce. Don't threaten cessation of supplies unless you really mean it.
3. For any threats you do make, always give a clear date - "Unless payment is received at this office by noon on 22 June we shall be forced to suspend the processing of your materials".

4. Always be polite, even when making threats. Avoid statements like, "In all my years in business I have never come across such an

outrageous attempt to avoid paying legitimate bills, and I can tell you that my colleagues in the Chamber of Commerce will hear about this..." Instead, no matter what the provocation, state simply that, "I am most sorry that we have not been able to reach a settlement, and it is with great regret that I must inform you that on June 22 I shall be forced to take this matter to the County Court unless an agreement is reached before then."

TRADE CREDIT

When you buy goods from other businesses you will normally expect to be given an invoice which you then pay a month or so later. Obviously if you can delay payment for more than a month then you are in effect getting extra interest-free credit.

To extend the trade credit you get needs a feel for judging which creditors you can delay paying without harming your own position. Here are two contrasting examples: On the one hand British Telecom. Fail to pay your phone bill and your phone lines will be disconnected, which could well spell disaster for your business. Consider on the other hand a magazine in which you advertise your services. The magazine publisher will know that if he pushes you too hard you may pay up but refuse to advertise again. Quite probably he will prefer to have you advertising repeatedly but paying late rather than advertising just once but paying on time.

If you can get such judgements right you could hold back on sufficient money to reduce your overdraft radically.

VAT RETURNS

Most businesses pay Customs and Excise VAT every quarter, the amount being the difference between the VAT they have paid out to other businesses, and the VAT included in their sales. If the business is making a profit then sales are larger than costs and so the VAT collected is larger than the VAT paid, and hence a payment to Customs is due. (This is not true in the case of businesses which deal largely in zero rated goods of course).

VAT returns have to be made by specific dates - pay late and you can end up being charged interest, or even fined. For example, you may be asked to account for three months VAT to 31 March no later than 30 April. This means that if you issue an invoice on 31 March for 1000 plus 150 VAT, that 150 will have to be sent to Customs and Excise no later than 30 April. However if that invoice were delayed by just one day, to 1 April, it would fall into the next VAT collecting period (1 April to 30 June), and that would be payable by 31 July. In other words that 150 would stay in your bank account for an extra three months.

Purchasing. You may spend £100,000 a year on your business - a 10% saving all round would reduce your borrowing requirement by £10,000 at a stroke. Obviously if you are totally tied to the franchisor for purchases there is nothing you can do on this point, but where you have flexibility spend some time looking at the options. Don't buy in poor-quality materials, but do try and negotiate the best deal for your company. There are circumstances in which everything from paperclips to computers can be reduced in price, possibly because of the salesman's need to make a sale, or because of your willingness to pay on time, or because of the competitiveness of the market place.

Do not accept list prices when buying for your business - everything is negotiable.

ACCOUNTANCY, FINANCE AND THE FRANCHISOR

Taking up a franchise is a costly business, not only because of the franchise fee, but also because of the money you must spend on premises, equipment and so on. If soon after you have invested all this money the franchisor moves into liquidation, you may find yourself not only losing your franchise fee, but also having several expensive legal commitments in terms of leases which are of no use to you, and cannot be easily disposed of.

With this in mind you should consider consulting an accountant before you sign the franchise agreement so that he can explain his view of the financial stability or otherwise of the franchisor. You should also take the time to learn a few basic accounting techniques yourself so that you can more fully evaluate the propositions that are being put to you. Since you are going to need to be able to prepare basic management accounts once you have started trading, and since you will need an accountant to help prepare your annual accounts, it could be a false economy not to take professional advice from the start.

Undertake some preliminary work yourself - you may be surprised to find out just how much you can discover through working on figures which will be widely available to you. What is more such an exercise will not only tell you about the franchisor, but also be good practice for later since all the analyses that you perform on the figures of the franchisor will need to be done on your own business once you are up and trading.

In order to make judgements of a financial nature you need clear financial information, and the obvious source of this is the franchisor. Whilst you should not expect a franchisor to hand out this sort of information to every enquirer, once you have established your own serious interest in the franchise you should expect a positive attitude from the franchisor. Helpful responses will indicate a franchisor with nothing to hide. Anything else and it may be either that the franchisor's business is itself not very sound financially, or that the franchisor is generally secretive and unhelpful. Either way evasive answers on financial matters will also suggest that the financial projections made for the franchise itself may have to be taken with a pinch of salt! Further, if secrecy is a key part of the franchisor's style then you may wonder how you will fare in getting help and information from the franchisor once you start as a franchisee, and you may also wonder what sort of publicity and promotion is going to be arranged on your behalf when you launch.

The first thing you need is a set of annual accounts from the franchisor. If the franchisor is a limited company (and the vast majority of them are) then audited accounts have to be lodged with Companies House and these can be inspected. Since the accounts are in the public domain there is clearly no reason why the franchisor should not send you a photocopy. Partnerships and sole traders (i.e. those firms without the letters Ltd or PLC at the end of their name) do not have to submit accounts to Companies House, but nevertheless must have accounts prepared for the Inland Revenue, and again ought to be willing to supply information before they take your money.

You should not imagine that in studying the accounts all you are looking for is the level of profit being made by the franchisor. A franchisor who makes an enormous profit may do so at the expense of the franchisees who are getting a raw deal. Indeed in the worst of situations a large profit might mean the franchisor is running an operation in which he takes a big franchise fee, offers little support, allows the franchisee to go into liquidation, and then sells the franchise again for a large sum.

A franchisor who is losing money may be one who is in serious trouble, but may alternatively be one who is assiduously putting the best interests of the franchisees first, ensuring that they are soundly based and supported before seeking to make profits for the franchisor.

PROJECTIONS.

If the franchisor has suggested that he will have 50 franchisees in place by a specific date it is worth looking to see if that projection was fulfilled. If not, you may wish to ask why, and if you are not satisfied with the answer you may wish to take other forecasts with some reluctance.

GROWTH RATE

At the same time you may note just how many franchisees there are this year as compared with last year. Of course if the franchise is nearing the completion of the national network the number may be static, yet a franchise with a projected total level of 100 franchisees, but which for three years has been hovering at only half that number may be in difficulties. Why is it failing to complete the national network? On the face of it, it would seem to be to everyone's advantage to have the network complete. To all such questions there may be perfectly reasonable answers - for example a desire to ensure that only the most able and competent of franchisees are appointed.

If your research backs this up all well and good. If not, ask more questions and take even greater care.

COMPARISONS

Comparisons should be made between the franchise you are considering and other franchises within the same area of work, with other franchises in general, and with non-franchised businesses in this sphere of work.

ASSETS AND LIABILITIES

Companies have two sorts of assets - fixed and current. Fixed assets are the machines, fixtures and fittings that are used to operate your business. For example if you have a computer to help you do your accounts that is a fixed asset. Current assets are those that relate to the very nature of your business. If you have a computer in stock because you deal in computers that is a current asset.

The current assets also include the money you are owed by debtors (for example people you have recently invoiced but have not yet received money from) and any cash you have. From this you take away the current liabilities - the money you owe other people for items you have bought but not yet paid for and of course the bank overdraft (but not long-term loans which are being repaid over a fixed period). Here's how the sum works in practice:

Fixed assets	**20,000.00**
Current assets	
Stock at cost	8,000.00
Debtors	12,000.00
Cash	1,000.00
Total current	21,000.00
Current liabilities	
Creditors	11,000.00
Overdraft	4,000.00
Total liabilities	15,000.00

Therefore current assets less current liabilities = £21,000 - £15,000 = £6,000.

The total assets of the company is the sum of the current assets (£6,000) and the Fixed assets (£20,000) - in this case £26,000

All companies should have positive figures both for the fixed assets and for the current assets. Take a look at the latest year's figures compared with last year's. If there is a major change there may be a good reason, but generally speaking a sudden drop in assets means something is going wrong.

You should also use these figures to calculate this simple sum:

CURRENT ASSETS

CURRENT LIABILITIES

Since, as we have said the assets should exceed the liabilities, we should have a positive number here. However a very high number (above 3 for example) may mean that far too much money is tied up in the business in an unproductive way. Remember that the current assets are mostly made up of people who owe the firm money, and stock. If the firm is owed a tremendous amount (compared to its size) it may be that it is inefficient in getting money in (or worse, it may be including in its list of debts money which it knows realistically it has no chance of ever reclaiming). Likewise if the stock value is higher than it needs to be the company is either being inefficient in controlling its stock levels or is deliberately overestimating the value of its stock in order to make its books look better.

RETURN ON CAPITAL EMPLOYED

All businesses have two things in common - they have money tied up in them, and they aim to make a profit. Obviously if you have capital available you can invest it in fairly safe institutions. Invest £20,000 in a Building Society account and you will get a regular rate of return. The percentage return on your capital will vary according to the market situation, but you will be sure that barring the total collapse of the economic system your money is fairly safe.

Let us say for the sake of argument the current interest rate paid by building societies is 10%. The question is, if you put your money into a business will it earn you a lot more? It certainly ought to since investing in business (your own or anyone else's) is a gamble - if things go wrong you can certainly lose all your money.

The amount of capital invested in a company is usually made up of share capital (the money invested by the owners of the company) and loan capital. Add these together and you get the capital employed.

To work out the return on capital employed simply do the following sum:

$$\frac{\text{PROFIT}}{\text{CAPITAL EMPLOYED}}$$

For example if the profit is 10,000 and the capital within the business is 50,000 the answer to the equation is 1/5 or 20% - double the rate of return from the building society.

In general the return on capital employed should increase year on year, although of course there may be exceptional years where particular problems or major investment programmes result in a temporary downturn.

I have already mentioned that the capital within a business consists of share capital and loan capital. What you next need to consider is the relationship between the two - that is how much money has come from outside sources in terms of loans (for example from the bank) and how much from the owners of the business. In this case we do this sum:

LOAN CAPITAL
_____

SHARE CAPITAL

If a man sets up a business in which he invests 10,000 (that is the share capital) and the bank puts in 10,000 (the loan capital) the sum clearly comes out at 1/1. The answer is usually expressed as a ratio 1:1.

However if he invests 15,000 himself and only asks the bank for 5000 the sum works as

$$\frac{5000}{15000} = \frac{1}{3}$$

or as a ratio 1:3

On the other hand if he invests 10,000 himself but persuades the bank to lend him 50,000 the sum is now

$$\frac{50,000}{10,000}$$

or as a ratio 5:1.

This could spell serious trouble for the business. Since so much money is now borrowed from the bank it may not be possible to pay all the interest payments, or repay the full debt on time. In other words the profits of the company are unlikely to be enough to pay the interest due to the bank. A ratio of 4:1 or more spells great danger, and if you spot anything remotely like that you should start asking serious questions about the franchisor's business. If the franchisor suggests that you should set up your business with a gearing of anything over 3:1 it may be that the franchisor is anxious to get franchisees set up at any price, and may not worry how quickly they will be shut down.

CONSIDERING YOUR OWN FRANCHISE

Having examined the finances of the franchisor it is time to examine in detail the finances for the proposed franchise you are thinking of taking up. What you must have by this stage is a clear inventory of everything that is required for you to start operating, and by everything we mean everything down to the office stationery, typewriter, heater and the first tank full of petrol. The details will of course vary but should include all the equipment you will need not only to produce the goods or service you will deal in but also to run the general administration. There should also be full details of building costs covering every aspect of the building from conversion costs through to painting the sign over the door, from paying the architect to paying British Telecom for installing the phone system.

Next there should be everything to do with the franchise itself - including your own legal expenses, accountancy expenses and VAT. This last item is often forgotten, for although it is true that as a registered business the VAT on your set-up costs will eventually be reclaimed from Customs and Excise, this can take time, and the reclaiming may come long after you have had to pay the money.

From all these figures you should get details of exactly how much money is required. Some will then be discounted as part of any leasing agreements, but the rest will have to be provided partly by yourself and partly by the bank or other financial institutions. Most franchises who have given information on the subject suggest that about 66% of total costs (excluding anything that is leased of course) can be provided by the bank - and this seems a reasonable figure to work on. In other words you will need to provide one third of the total expenditure. This one third has to be available at the start of the franchise as liquid capital - you should have it in the form of money held in a bank, building society or similar institution ready for the moment you have to pay it out.

Indeed looking at finances in this way is a reasonable way of thinking what you might be able to afford. If you have £10,000 in a bank, perhaps saved from redundancy pay, or from selling your last business, then there is probably little point looking at any franchise which has a total set-up cost estimated at over £30,000.

In addition to these set-up costs you should also consider the day-to-day costs you will incur during the first few months of business, before you start getting much money in. The franchisor should certainly give you an indication of how much money you are likely to need to get you through these opening months. This money is normally provided in terms of an overdraft, but do not be led to believe the overdraft can be used for anything other than day-to-day expenses. If you negotiate an overdraft with your bank, and then use it to finance the buying of a car, you are liable to find the overdraft called in very rapidly.

Having worked out the initial capital outlay you will next want to check the projected profit for the company based on the income and expenditure for each of the first three years. You need to know if the figures from which the profit is derived are reasonable. Do this in two ways: through looking at the figures yourself and asking yourself if they look reasonable, and by speaking to franchisees and asking if they are making the sort of money projected.

It is quite possible to check any figures you are given in elementary ways. For example, let us imagine you are thinking of taking on a fast print franchise which specialises in off-high street sites.

You can check the following:

Income
Watch the number of people going in and out of a print shop. Are they all customers, or are some just making enquiries? What do you think is the average cost of their printing work? (Such information should be available either from the franchisor or a nearby franchisee). From this information you can get a rough estimate of the turnover your shop might have.

The Rent
If any premises in the area in which your franchise might be situated are available, enquire of the estate agents what the rental is. If none are available, go into a few agents, tell them what you are looking for, and ask what sort of rent you might be expected to pay.

Wages
Walk into any print shop and count the number of staff. Next pick up the local paper and look under Situations Vacant for any printing jobs and shop reception jobs. From this you can work out the weekly salary bill of the shop, which multiplied by 52 will give the annual bill. Is your estimate close to that shown in the franchisor figures? If not why not? (If you can't work out why not put the figures to the franchisor and ask why. Then ask yourself if his explanation is reasonable).

However despite all these calculations it is possible that something will go very wrong, and that you may find that you are seriously under-capitalised. The problem might be a lower than expected turnover or higher than expected costs. Whatever the reason you have either to solve the problem, or sell up possibly at an enormous loss to yourself. It is particularly galling if you do find yourself forced to sell out at a loss when you are sure that if only you could lay your hands on another few thousand pounds you would not only rescue the business, but also develop it into a very successful venture. So it is not a bad idea to consider what you will do if things do go wrong.

The most obvious solution is to return to the bank for more funds, although this can lead to a problem if gearing gets too high, as we have already noted. Alternatively you may be able to dig deeper into your own pocket or that of relatives. You may even contemplate selling your house and moving into something smaller in order to raise some funds.

If all this seems hopelessly drastic, it shows the value of having some funds in reserve, just in case. Borrowing to your ultimate limit in order to launch any business, franchised or otherwise, is generally not a good idea.

CHAPTER 6

EMPLOYING PEOPLE

There are a number of franchises which can be operated as "one man bands". Many involve running vans stocked up with motor trade items, video tapes or anything else that can be sold from a van, while others involve working from home on a part-time basis. All other franchises include, as part of the operation, employing people from the very beginning of the operation.

Both types of franchise have their advantages and disadvantages and it is important to be clear on these before making a decision on which way you wish to go as a franchisee.

THE ONE MAN BAND

ADVANTAGES:

You are your own master (leaving aside the franchisor of course). On day-to-day affairs you do things your way, and answer to no one.

Most people agree that staff can be a problem, especially when they take time off, arrive late, have babies or otherwise fail to do a day's work.

Staff cost money - not just in pay but in National Insurance Contributions, holiday pay, sick pay and the like.

Staff need space - having staff makes it much harder for you to work from home.

DISADVANTAGES:

If you are taken sick the business effectively comes to a halt. You may be healthy now, but no one can foresee all eventualities.

When you go on holiday you must either take on a relief operator (and such a person can be very hard to find) or else shut down for a week or two. Such shutdowns can be very disruptive for your business - people expect you to be available when they want you, and if you are not they will surely go elsewhere.

There is a limit to what you can do - without staff you cannot expand.

THE FRANCHISEE WITH STAFF

ADVANTAGES:

No problems with holidays, your illnesses, or expansion.

Very good staff can be trained to take over the business leaving you in the role of chairman - overseeing but not actually getting your hands dirty. There is nothing like making money without doing too much work.

DISADVANTAGES:

Staff need space to work in - which means rents and rates add to the cost of salaries.

Staff come and go - you will always be trying to recruit more people.

The law is very detailed on what you can and can't do with your staff. You need to be well-informed.

All in all, if you do want to take on some employees you will need to know how to go about finding staff, how to select staff, how to handle staff once employed, along with the legal obligations of employment, from the very start.

What follows is a brief summary of some of the major points you ought to follow when employing people.

LOCATING POSSIBLE STAFF

It can be astonishingly difficult to locate suitable staff in certain parts of the country, and if you have no experience of selecting staff in your area do not automatically assume that a high level of unemployment actually means that the right people are available for work.

When seeking staff you have the following options:

GOVERNMENT SCHEMES

At the time of writing the Youth Training Scheme (YTS) and Employment Training (ET) are both operative and can supply staff in some cases. The advantage to you is that the amount you have to pay the staff is often quite small, and if you do get a good employee you can then retain that person at the end of the training and give him or her a full time job and a suitable salary.

YTS trainees normally come to the YTS scheme straight from school, having left with limited qualifications. ET trainees are normally older people who have been out of work for some years and are seeking a gradual re-introduction to the working environment. The theory is that such people often lack confidence and therefore need support and guidance as they come back into the world of work. In both cases the trainees will be away from their job one or two days a week to undergo training at college.

If you wish to register a vacancy for either YTS or ET trainees contact your local job centre and ask for details of the local offices handling the trainees. They will then interview you to discuss the implications of taking on a trainee, and put your registration on file. But be warned, it is quite possible to register and then not have an applicant for your post for months or years on end.

LOCAL SCHOOLS

If you are interested in taking on school leavers at the age of 16 or 18 write to the secondary schools in your area with full details of the job, addressing your letter to the Head of Careers. The best time to write is immediately after Easter in order to catch those who plan to leave at the end of the summer term. While not all schools are co-operative many will have a noticeboard showing local job opportunities, and will help in getting the right person to apply for your job.

CAREERS OFFICES

Careers offices help young people who have recently left school to find work which will meet their particular requirements. They try and help youngsters who may be bemused by the world of work, and who are possibly unsure of what they ought to be doing. Careers Offices support the work of careers teachers in schools but do not seek to become involved directly with children who are still attending school.

JOB CENTRE

Registering of vacancies at the Job Centre can be done on the phone, and costs nothing. Not everyone put forward for interviews by a local Job Centre is actually willing to take on work, and some who apply for jobs are hardly suitable. But it is still possible to find good staff via a Job Centre, and it is always worth registering a vacancy.

NEWSPAPER ADVERTISING

Local daily newspapers and weekly paid-for and free papers all carry large numbers of job advertisements. Advertisements can be phoned in - but look at the paper first and decide exactly what you want to say before you make the call. Do not be pushed into taking large box advertisements or long advertising runs lasting several days or more without trying a one-off advertisement first.

Even in the smallest of advertisements try and make your announcement stand out. The advertisement: "Book packer required, Northampton" sounds bleak. But "Book packer wanted to work with friendly young team in smoke-free office in Northampton" will only cost a few pounds more in a local daily, but is likely to get a better response.

MAGAZINE ADVERTISING

This is normally only worthwhile when seeking well-paid qualified senior staff in a particular industry. But the lead up time to advertisements can be quite long on monthly publications, so plan well in advance.

EMPLOYMENT AGENCIES

Employment Agencies are controlled by law; make sure any Agency that you deal with has a Department of Employment registration number on its headed paper. The agencies charge the employer for finding staff - usually on a no-find, no-fee basis. Normal charges range between 3% and 10% of one year's salary - and there is only limited recompense if the person resigns soon after taking on the job.

EMPLOYMENT AND THE LAW

In general terms the law sets out the following obligations on anyone who employs staff.

You have to abide by the law of the land, including of course all employment law regarding safety, insurances, equal pay, racial discrimination, employment of children and the like. Ignorance of legislation is no excuse if you are caught breaking it.

You have to provide your staff with reasonable and safe working conditions and pay your staff for work done. In return your staff have to undertake the work given, do it with care, and not betray trust by giving away company secrets to other firms. You don't have to provide your staff with work - they cannot complain if they are paid but have to sit around doing nothing!

You should, but you don't have to, provide a contract of employment along with work rules and disciplinary codes. Obviously if you are working in a small office with just two or three staff, handing out detailed disciplinary codes may do nothing other than alienate the workers, but it is still worth having a written contract. If you choose not to offer a written contract you must supply a written summary of the work to be undertaken.

You must provide a brief written analysis of how pay is calculated when wages are paid out, including statements concerning the deduction of income tax and national insurance contributions.

You must allow your staff to take as paid holidays all public holidays unless you give them a contract specifying otherwise. Other holidays are a matter for your agreement with your staff.

Dismissing unwanted staff is often a matter of concern, and there is a popular belief that it is impossible to dismiss anyone once you have taken them on. In fact this is quite untrue. Removing people from their job is covered by unfair dismissal legislation, but very large numbers of employees are specifically excluded from the legislation, and it is always worth being very sure of your ground before you take anyone on.

The first point to note is that anyone who has worked for you for less than two years full time is not covered by unfair dismissal legislation - you can dismiss them without giving any reason, and merely have to give one week's notice, or one week's pay in lieu of notice. If you employ a person for between 8 and 16 hours a week then the person has to work for five years to be able to enter a claim under unfair dismissal legislation. Less than eight hours a week and once again you have the freedom to dismiss as you wish.

Having said that, anyone employed by you, even if for under eight hours a week, can have recourse to the law for dismissal on racial, sexual or religious grounds. In fact, the legislation against discrimination on racial sexual and religious grounds overrides the unfair dismissal legislation in all cases irrespective of any other factors.

Among the other exclusions from entitlement to claim unfair dismissal is anyone over retirement age and also anyone whose contract itself contains some element of illegality, (such as an agreement to pay part of the wage in cash and not declare it to the Inland Revenue).

If you do have an employee who has worked with you long enough to be within the unfair dismissal legislation, then you have to give good reason for dismissal. This normally involves at least one of the following:

Misconduct, such as not doing what is asked, arriving late, being dishonest, or being violent, drunk or abusive. But you should not be tempted to think that one example of any of the above is enough for dismissal. If an employee works well but looks moody, refuses to join in the general banter of the office, very occasionally turns up late, or is once or twice a year a little tipsy in the afternoon then that is not normally considered sufficient grounds dismissal. More serious offences however can constitute grounds for immediate dismissal, such as serious violence, or any form of theft or blatant dishonesty within the business. Likewise if an employee is obviously unable to do the job for which he or she is appointed the employee can be sacked - as for example in the case of a driver who loses his driving licence.

Although certain types of behaviour (most notably dishonesty or theft) can constitute grounds for instant dismissal, it is often the case that you will be obliged to warn an employee that his or her work is not satisfactory. In such cases you should ensure that you keep strict and accurate records of both the behaviour which leads to the warnings and the way the warnings themselves are handled.

There is no set pattern to the way warnings should be given but you may wish to start by giving the employee a mild, perhaps even friendly, warning along the lines of "I know its not like you, and I am sure it won't happen again, but I felt I ought to say that..." Note down the offence, the gist of your comments, and the date.

If the behaviour persists, a more formal spoken warning might be given along the lines that, "If it happens again, I will have to give you a written warning..." After that might come a written warning, which itself should include reference to the two previous spoken warnings, with dates, and the information that should the offence occur again within the next three months (or whatever time is seen to be appropriate) the employee will be dismissed with one week's notice.

If dismissal does occur, do put it in writing, and refer to the previous letter and warnings, again giving dates. In this way you will make it clear to your employee that you have been keeping exact notes, and that the employee, who has probably not kept notes, is unlikely to succeed with any unfair dismissal claim.

An employee who goes sick however may be able to claim unfair dismissal if sacked - the exact position will depend on the nature and length of the illness. But remember, if you employ someone who starts taking time off for illness during his or her first two years, you can legally dismiss that person without having to give any reason.

Throughout the difficult situation of removing someone from your employ, you should ensure that you as employer behave reasonably and explain your views clearly, and in writing, to the employee. Although you are not obliged to give reasons for dismissal, it is often helpful to do so, especially if you feel there is any chance that the employee might claim that the real motive was religious or racial bias. Your franchisor should also help with further details of what you can and cannot do.

Dismissing staff is an appalling waste of time and money. The process is liable to cost you a week's wages with no work done, and you will also need to re-train each new employee you bring in. There will also be the cost of advertising for new staff, and the inevitable disruption caused by having a vacancy, even if it is filled within one day.

Obviously it is much better if you can avoid getting into the situation in which you have to dismiss staff in the first place, and in order to do this you might find the following ideas helpful in your search for the perfect employee who will loyally stay by your side until one of you retires.

Firstly, do not expect too much. The business is yours - it is your money on the line (and possibly your house too). So you will be prepared to work morning noon and night to get it right. But it is unfair to expect your average employee on an average wage to do this. Likewise do not expect average employees to understand exactly what you want them to do if you do not explain it fully. When setting tasks, go into detail first time round. Assume no prior knowledge with junior staff.

Secondly, deal with any problems from the start. If an employee turns up late on the second day, point out the misdemeanours there and then. Do not give the benefit of the doubt over and over again, when a friendly word could bring the matter to clarification more rapidly.

Thirdly, reward good staff as rapidly as you can with pay rises, improved conditions and so on. Everyone says that good staff are hard to find - when you do get them remember their needs. The best way to keep staff is to treat them well. You can encourage good staff by being very open about your business. Let them know what is going on, how things are working out, if the business is succeeding or failing and so on. The more your staff feel you are taking them into your confidence the more they will respond to you, and the better the quality of their work will be.

Lastly, a special word about school leavers. School leavers come in all shapes and sizes. There are those who nervously wonder what working is going to be all about and who will do anything and everything you tell them. There are those who are so used to treating teachers with contempt that they will treat you in the same way. Some will be bullied by parents who feel they are not doing enough for themselves, and will tell you on day 2 that, "My Dad says that I am entitled to a 15 minute tea break every morning and afternoon," and there are those who find it impossible to use their initiative or common sense in anything.

Your task when employing school leavers is to decide as quickly as possible what sort of person you have got. Unless you are convinced that it is your role in life to train the untrainable, get rid of those who refuse to give an honest day's work and concentrate on bringing the best out of the rest. But always recognise that the good ones need time to settle down and sort themselves out. Give them time. Remember you may be employing someone who has done nothing for the past ten years except sit behind a desk and write down what the teacher said: adjusting to the world of work can be a traumatic experience.

CONSIDERING A FRANCHISE OPPORTUNITY?

Consult a solicitor who is familiar with the franchise market.
Call Ray Walley
Franchise Partner, an Associate of
British Franchise Association

Mundays

S O L I C I T O R S

The Bellbourne
103 High Street
Esher,
Surrey, KT10 9QF
Tel: 0372 67272
Fax: 0372 63782
Telex: 897742

Also at:
Fox House
44 High Street
Cobham,
Surrey KT11 3EB
Tel: 0932 68345
Fax: 0932 68685
Telex: 897742

Speer House
40 The Parade
Claygate
Esher
Surrey, KT10 0NY
Tel: 0372 67272
Fax: 0372 68850
Telex: 897742

Fleetwood
3 Bath Passage
(Adjacent Guildhall)
Kingston upon Thames
Surrey, KT1 1ES
Tel: 01-547 3533
Fax: 01-547 1265
Telex: 897742

CHAPTER 7

LEGAL
IMPLICATIONS

WHAT SORT OF COMPANY?

Many franchise agreements stipulate that the franchisee must set up a limited company before trading commences, and that all the trading of the franchisee must pass through that company.

However, less expensive franchises often omit such a clause in the contract and if you are looking at a franchise that does not carry such a stipulation you then have the choice between three legal types of company: a sole trader, a partnership, and the limited company.

The term sole trader is somewhat misleading, for it does not refer to a person working alone, but rather to a person who is the full legal owner of the business. Such a person takes full responsibility for the profits and losses of the business, and has no separate company to protect himself if things go wrong. Put another way, in legal terms the sole trader and the business are all one. If, in the worst possible scenario the sole trader commits some dreadful indiscretion in the business and is sued for a large amount of money, it is he himself who is sued. If the courts find against him he has to come up with the money, even if it means selling his house, business, furniture and everything else.

Against this there are the advantages of having total control over the business, having few legal requirements to follow, and in some cases a more liberal tax regime than might otherwise be the case with a limited company.

ADLERS

THE Franchise Team:

MARTIN MENDELSOHN
MANZOOR ISHANI
ROBERT KING
JEREMY JACOBS
MARK PETERS
MARTIN OMMANNEY

Combining over a half century of Franchising experience

Solicitors:
22-26 Paul Street
London EC2A 4JH
Telephone: 01-481 9100
Telex: 883831
Telefax: 01-247 4701 (Groups 2 & 3)
Document Exchanges: London-LDE 107: City CDE 107
Cables: Tutissimus London EC2

The one way to protect yourself against major losses is to make sure that you have very few assets - typically a businessman or woman might transfer ownership of house, cars, savings and the like to a non- trading spouse. But then you have to think how much you trust your spouse!

In a legal sense partnerships are similar to sole traders except that each partner benefits from the others' input, and suffers for their mistakes. Partnerships are often set up when two or more people come together to pool money for the launch of the business, or when each has a particular area of expertise or experience, or when it is important to have a senior person on the premises at all times. A partnership helps to share out the responsibility and allows each partner to go on holiday knowing there is someone responsible in charge.

Partnership agreements are normally written out in detail and signed by the partners at the start of the business - if they are not then there is a 19th century act which covers the business in general terms. Certainly if you do not want exactly equal ownership and sharing by the partners then you must write out the agreement.

The biggest problem with partnerships is that if one of the partners makes a mistake then all the partners suffer. At worst if one of the partners ties up a bad deal which loses the partnership hundreds of thousands of pounds then all the partners have to meet the obligation - which normally means each partner has to sell his or her house in order to realise the money. It is terrible enough to lose your own house through your own mistake, but to lose it through the mistake of your partner....

If matters go the other way and there are great profits to be made by the partnership then other problems may emerge. Many partnerships consist of one person who runs the shop and another who puts up the cash. After a while the person who put up the cash may have received all that money back from profits which have been paid to the partners as drawings. But the profits continue to mount through the hard work of the partner running the shop, and the non-working partner continues to draw money. It is not too hard to imagine a situation where after some five years of this, in which the non-working partner has had his money back three times over, the working partner begins to get a bit agitated. Each side will have a point - the non-working partner will stress that without his original input the business would not exist at all. The working partner stresses that when they started neither imagined there would be this much success, which is all down to his hard work. To overcome such an argument it may be better to avoid the problem totally by having the contract drawn up to include what will happen under extremes of profit and loss. And having drawn up such a document, do get a solicitor to have a good look at it.

The only legal restriction you have to avoid is that you must not have more than twenty partners in the partnership. With both the sole trader and the partnership there are no restrictions on the size of the business in terms of the number of staff or its turnover.

Finally the limited company, best known by its abbreviation "Ltd" which appears after the company's name. In full this abbreviation stands for "Limited liability" , which stresses that its liability to meet debts and other claims is limited to the assets of the business. In other words, unlike the business of the sole trader or partnership, the company is separated in law from its owner. (There are exceptions to this, as when the owners deliberately use the company in order to obtain goods and services knowing that they cannot be paid for, or when the directors are so incompetent that they simply do not know how the business is faring when they ought to have known, but for the most part this separation of the company from its owners holds true).

Clearly, no business is going to supply large amounts of services or goods on credit to another business without some guarantee, and therefore any major supplier (such as a bank which runs an overdraft for a limited company) will still require a guarantee - for example the directors' house - should the company fail. The limited liability protection is therefore only helpful in certain circumstances. If the company makes a major loss on a particular contract and ceases to trade owing money to the bank, then there is likely to be little protection for the directors. If however the money is owed to a variety of trade creditors, it is possible that there will be every protection for the directors, with the losses being borne by the small creditors as bad debts.

In return for the benefits granted to limited liability companies, the state expects certain formalities to be observed. All limited companies must have a registered address which must be recorded at Companies' House. This address need not be the trading address of the business, but it is its legal address, which means that limited companies should not disappear by moving from one place to another without leaving forwarding addresses.

Just as the registered address is recorded at Companies House so are copies of the company's accounts, and these are open to inspection by the public, so it is harder, although not impossible, to hide bad figures in a limited company. The most common ways of making bad accounts look better include:

Keeping in the accounts money owed from companies which are clearly never going to pay. So if you are owed £20,000 by various firms, but one of those firms is in the hands of the liquidators you really should remove that element from the current assets.

Increasing the value of the stock shown on the accounts beyond that which it should be. For example, if you make a product which has a new design each year, you will probably be left with a number of last year's model each January. Such items should probably be valued at a very low price, but you could put the value in the accounts at a very high level on the spurious grounds that the items now have scarcity value It is a clever trick, but once a firm starts using clever tricks to improve the state of its accounts it is fair to state that it may not be on a very straight path.

A limited company can have anything from two to 50 shareholders. As before there are no legal restrictions on its size in terms of staff or turnover. However the limited company must have two legal documents (the Memorandum and the Articles) and pay a registration fee. It must also present audited accounts each year. If you are about to start a limited company your accountant will help explain these documents to you.

TAXATION and NATIONAL INSURANCE

The sole trader and the partners within a partnership pay tax on the profit of the company, whether they draw it out or not. The partners are treated as self-employed people which means that their taxation is assessed at the end of the tax year and paid later.

Such self-employed people pay all their own national insurance and pension contributions, have no entitlement to sick pay, are ineligible for unemployment benefit, cannot claim redundancy payments and are liable for VAT (see below) if business turnover is sufficiently high.

Directors of limited companies are treated as employees for tax purposes, and they pay tax on a monthly basis as do other employees. Profits that remain within the company are then taxed under Corporation Tax. They also normally pay more in national insurance contributions.

If as a franchisee you are given the choice between being a limited company and being a partnership or a sole trader, you may find the advantages of each system fall out as follows:

Sole trader - lower accountancy costs, no set-up costs, lower taxation (unless you are making enough profits to bring you into higher rate tax bands), total vulnerability if something goes wrong.

Partnership - access to the finance and help of the partner, tax advantages of a sole trader, vulnerability of a sole trader, with the complication of being liable for your partners' losses and errors.

Limited company - some protection when things go wrong (but not where you have given guarantees), possibly higher tax rates, certainly higher accountancy charges, greater costs and formalities in setting up.

In all you may find it better to start as a sole trader or partnership and transfer to a limited company a little later.

VALUE ADDED TAX

Each year the Chancellor of the Exchequer sets a minimum level for VAT registration. Below that level of turnover companies have the choice of registering or not registering for VAT while above that level they must register. Where the business is a limited company it is that company which has the VAT registration. Where a sole trader or partnership operates, the registration is for that individual or collection of individuals.

Virtually all franchisees are obliged to register for VAT. In brief this implies the following:

On all goods and services VAT must be levied at the appropriate rate. In some cases (including at the time of writing newspapers, books, some items of clothing, food, some printing etc) this rate is zero. In all other cases the 1989 rate is 15%. What this means is that from the day you register your prices are suddenly raised by 15% - the customer has to pay that extra 15% to you but you do not get the benefit, for that money has to be forwarded to Customs and Excise - you do not get to keep it.

Clearly it is no advantage to you to charge your customers 15% extra if you do not get the benefit. But on the other side of the coin you do have the benefit of getting the VAT back when you buy goods and services. Thus if you purchase a tonne of steel, a set of computer disks, or a pack of paperclips you will be paying 15% VAT to the supplier. You can set that expense against the VAT payments you have received and so get a reduction in the money you owe Customs and Excise. In fact it is not unknown for firms to get refunds from Customs and Excise after their first few months of trading because they are buying in more goods than they are selling (especially as they are kitting out offices and factories).

There are just a few words of warning that need to be added: record keeping for Customs and Excise needs to be very exact - you must have a receipt for everything you purchase and must keep it neatly filed in date order pending an inspection from Customs and Excise. You must also keep records of every invoice you issue. And just in case you were thinking that this was a good way of saving money on a car, you cannot claim back the VAT paid on a car purchase (but you can on the petrol).

INLAND REVENUE

You will need to deal with the Inland Revenue over two matters - the payment of tax on your profits, and the payment of tax and national insurance on the staff you employ.

BUSINESS TAX

It is up to each trader, partnership or company to provide a set of accounts to the Inland Revenue, on the basis of which tax computations can be made. What many people do not realise that it is in fact normally necessary to set up two sets of accounts - one prepared in the normal way and the other prepared to meet the requirements of the Revenue. This is a highly complex area and it is vital you have an accountant to help you prepare your accounts - although you can do some helpful preparatory work yourself, mostly by keeping very clear records of everything you sell and everything you buy in, plus all your bank statements and cheque stubs (completed clearly and in detail).

But in general it is fair to say that your taxable profit is calculated roughly by taking your income and removing your expenses.

These expenses will include all the normal things that you buy day-by-day for your business (but not items which are bought wholly or partly for your personal benefit). Items which are deemed to be capital equipment are handled in different ways, and normally cannot be written against expenditure in one go. Some items are specifically not allowed by the Revenue - for example taking people out for a meal - others have to be treated in particular ways.

Franchisees should note that it is often possible to reduce taxation through employing one's husband or wife in the firm. Even part-time work can be tax efficient since one's spouse can earn several thousand pounds (which will reduce company profits) while not paying any tax (assuming he or she does not already have another job). However it must be pointed out that the individual concerned must actually be working in the business. If the spouse has another job however, there are still tax advantages which can be looked at. If your business makes a loss that loss can be taken from the profit of your spouse's income and so reduce your spouse's liability to tax. Unfortunately this does not work if you set up a limited company - only with partnerships and sole traders. With limited companies the losses can only be set off against future profits.

PERSONAL TAXATION AND NATIONAL INSURANCE

If you employ people - irrespective of whether your firm is a sole trader, a partnership or a limited company, you normally have to deduct tax and national insurance from the employees' pay.

Once again full details are complex and beyond the scope of this book, but your accountant or the Inland Revenue will help. What is more, different industries have their own special rules where particular issues arise - the building trade is one obvious example. What follows therefore should be taken only as a general rule.

A full record of payment should be kept for everyone you employ - including casual and part-time staff. The Inland Revenue will provide you with a wide range of booklets and charts to help you calculate tax - it looks daunting, but you will probably find that for everyday use most of these manuals are not required.

For each person you employ you need to have some details. These are normally given on a tax form P45 supplied by the individual's previous employer. If the employee does not have such a form because they have not had a previous job, have lost it, have several part-time jobs, or whatever, then you need to ask them to fill in a form P46. You should also have a form P15 to give them so that they can get their own affairs in order. Finally you will need to record all the payments and tax calculations on form P11.

Armed with those forms and the explanation books that the Inland Revenue supply, you should be able to deduct tax and national insurance contributions from each employee. You will also find that you, as employer, have to pay some of the national insurance contribution which cannot be reclaimed from the employee.

In terms of paying yourself, the way in which tax is deducted depends on the type of company you have. If you have a limited company you will pay yourself and deduct tax and national insurance as with any of your staff. If you are a sole trader or running a partnership you can pay yourself whatever you think your company can afford, without reference to tax, for taxation is paid only on the profit of the company (but note that payments to yourself are 'drawings' and are not counted against expenses - they are deemed to be drawn from your profits and so are taxable if you make a profit, where 'profit' includes these payments).

You may have the occasional problem with individuals who claim that they are self-employed. Although there are special circumstances within certain trades which your franchisor will advise you on, in general you should treat such claims with scepticism. If you set work for a person and set the rate for that work the chances are that the person is technically employed by you. It doesn't matter where the work is done, or indeed who provides the tools. If in doubt you should get such a matter resolved quickly by the Inland Revenue for if you employ a person on a self-employed basis who really should have tax deducted at source through PAYE you may find yourself, as employer, having to pay a large tax bill. It is not unknown for the Revenue to trace matters back for a number of years and demand tax payments for employees who have long since left your employ and from whom you have no chance of reclaiming the money. Remember as the employer it is up to you to get matters right - if in doubt deduct PAYE tax and National Insurance.

CHAPTER 8

THE CONTRACT

One of the most worrying tendencies that I see in my work as editor of THE GOOD FRANCHISE GUIDE among would-be franchisees is that of signing the franchise contract no matter what it says, on the grounds that everyone else signed it so it must be all right.

This is a foolish approach in my opinion. There should be no doubt that most franchise agreements are heavily biased in favour of the franchisor, for it is the franchisor who draws the contract up. Such agreements are normally presented on a take it or leave it basis. On the one hand this can be very annoying, especially if you are very keen on the franchise but consider that one or two particular clauses present a problem. However you should also be wary of any franchisor who is willing to negotiate over major clauses in his contract. You may ask yourself if the franchisor doesn't mind if it is there or not, why was that clause in the contract in the first place? Was it just put there to try and catch the unwary?

To be fair, franchisors often include clauses in order to help them deal with difficult situations which may arise only rarely. Thus if one franchisee in a hundred causes a problem through refusing to pay his royalties on time, a clause may be added which states that non- payment will be grounds for ending the contract. If another starts to use singularly unsuitable staff, the franchisor responds by adding a clause to all contracts which states that the franchisor has the right to insist upon suitable staff training (paid for by the franchisee of course) where it is deemed necessary.

The reality is that the franchisor has not the slightest intention of cancelling a franchise agreement every time a royalty cheque does not arrive on time - he may be very sympathetic indeed where a franchisee has particular problems over a downturn in trade, or a large bad debt.

Neither will the franchisor insist that all staff have to be trained by an outside agency; he certainly does not have the time to start organising staff training on a major scale. But he is reserving the right to do just that so he can cope with extreme situations. What you as a potential franchisee have to judge is how likely the franchisor is to be sympathetic and understanding to individual cases - and this is a very hard judgement to make. The franchisor may say to you "that's only used in very rare cases" but the fact remains that the clause is in the contract and can be used no matter what verbal promises are made to the contrary. Remember also that in a business-to-business contract of this sort, much of the legislation to protect the general public against the imposition of "unfair terms" in contracts is not available. The law takes the view that businesses need to be comparatively free to negotiate deals of all types without the encumbrance of protective legislation, for while a member of the public may, through inexperience, get caught out in dealings with an unscrupulous trader, the businessman with his access to legal and financial consultants, should be able to spot problems before they occur.

The problem for you is that if this is your first venture into the business world you may find yourself accepting something that really ought not to be accepted. The rule for all contracts must be firstly to get legal advice and secondly talk to as many other franchisees who have signed that contract as possible.

All franchise agreements differ, but in general terms most include the following:

1. AN AGREEMENT TO BUY
THE FRANCHISE FOR A GIVEN AMOUNT

This section should incorporate specific opt-out clauses which will apply if certain things do or do not happen. For example, if the franchisee is unable to find a site that is suitable, the franchise obviously cannot proceed. Clearly it is then necessary to stop proceedings and refund any money so far paid.

Franchisee note:

If there is no site clause, do not sign.

2. A SPECIFICATION OF THE ACTIVITY

This sets down such basic factors as the area to be covered, the royalties, the fees, and what each side to the agreement will do. Much of this will be straightforward - you will know long before you reach this stage what the royalty payment is to be.

Franchisee note:

Watch out for clauses which show the circumstances under + which the royalty payment can be increased. Can it be increased for example at the franchisor's demand, with a certain amount of notice, or must the franchisor get the ok of each franchisee first? (I recently came across one franchise in which the franchisor was obliged to get franchisee permission to increase the royalty. Wanting to do so he invited all franchisees to London, spun a hard luck story about franchisor losses, and how the whole operation would fold if the royalty percentage did not rise, and then suggested the franchisees discuss the matter over lunch. After lunch the franchisees repaired to the bar, and after an hour or so boozing all save one signed away another 2% of their turnover. The one who did not sign is now enjoying the same support services from this nationally known franchise but paying less in royalties than everyone else.)

You should also look for any technical points on how the royalty itself is calculated. Is it strictly on turnover? If so, are you happy that your turnover will relate to your profit? Are you sure that you will not have elements within your business which themselves contribute to turnover without contributing much to profit? In addition if you find yourself slipping behind with royalty payments, you may find that you will be penalised through having to pay interest on the outstanding amount. This in itself may not seem too unreasonable, but you should check what interest rate you are going to have to pay.

3. CESSATION OF TRADE AGREEMENTS

How and when the franchisor can remove the franchisee's right to trade, and the level of compensation that will be provided (if any).

Franchisee note:

The franchisor may well say that he will never demand the closure of a franchisee's operation unless it is absolutely necessary due to the franchisee spoiling the good name of the whole operation. That may sound perfectly reasonable - but beware! There is an agreement attached to one widely available franchise that says the franchisor can terminate an agreement without compensation with just one week's notice without having to give the reason! Despite the obviously unjust nature of such a clause it would appear that many franchisees have willingly signed this agreement.

There will probably also be a clause in which the franchisor demands the right to approve any transfer to another franchisee; this will often be combined with a demand that no transfer can be effected while any outstanding debts remain. If you are selling when in financial difficulty this can be a problem.

Some franchise agreements also include low turnover clauses through which the franchisor can arbitrarily terminate the agreement simply because minimum sales are not met. While this is perhaps a preferable version of the clause which demands you take a certain amount of stock each month irrespective of your ability to sell it, you may wish to reflect upon the minima that are set in the contract, and ask if they are reasonable. (see point 16 below).

For example, in extreme conditions you may find yourself facing bankruptcy. In such circumstances the receiver will seek to realise such assets as you have in order to pay off the debts. However what you may find is that under such circumstances the franchisor has the right to dissolve the franchise agreement without compensation, and may even reserve certain rights in respect of the lease on the building, the equipment and any money you receive! In other words, at your worst moment the franchisor steps in and makes it worse still.

While no one is likely not to sign an agreement because he or she does not like the insolvency rules, you should refer back to your contract at the earliest moment things start going wrong. It may be better to cut your losses earlier rather than later.

You also may not be aware that the franchise agreement is for a set number of years. What are the renewal terms? Are you given enough time to make a reasonable amount of money and earn back the set-up costs? What happens to your equipment at the end of the term? Do all the leasing agreements run for the same length of time as the franchise agreement? If not, what are you supposed to do for premises in the last year of your agreement if the shop lease terminates one year prior to the franchise agreement?

4. RESTRICTIONS ON TRADE NOTICES

The franchisor may specify a wide range of activities you are and are not allowed to undertake during, and in the years following your operation of the franchise.

Franchisee note:
If you do open up other lines of business are you to pay a royalty on them also? Because you will be thinking mostly about the actual franchise itself you may not immediately consider developing into other areas, but a minor detail such as this can become something of importance after you have been running the business for a few years and feel the need to explore new fields.

5. PAYMENT OF ROYALTY IS NORMALLY BASED ON TURNOVER
The contract should define the meaning of turnover.

Franchisee note:
If the franchise deals with other businesses, then much of the work done will be done on credit. If this is so there will at some time or another be bad debts. They might occur as a result of firms that deliberately seek to defraud you, or through firms that become bankrupt and from whom you cannot get any money.

There may also be a few cases of firms who claim that the work you have done for them was not up to specification and therefore they will not pay all of the invoice.

Obviously in all cases such as these the loss of money that is due to you is bad enough, but if you then find that you have to pay a royalty on money that you have never received that can be too much! Check carefully - is the money to be paid on invoices issued or income received?

There is also the question of extra royalties which may be levied when required. Normally such additional funds are used for national advertising. If this is the case is there any restriction on how much can be levied, when it can be levied, and what is done with it?

6. REQUIREMENTS OF SERVICE
Some franchise agreements will state that the franchisee must provide himself with a suitable car. Others will specify what that vehicle must be.

Franchisee note:
Add up the costs of everything mentioned - including monthly lease repayments. It is very easy to underestimate just how much running a car and paying for a lease on it can cost you.

7. TERRITORY

The franchise will normally state specifically the range of your area for trading, or the area in which the franchisor agrees not to open another outlet.

Franchisee note:

Does the franchisor agree to do anything should another franchisee start trading in your area contrary to the agreement? It is all very well saying that each franchisee is given a specific area, but does the franchisor promise in your agreement to stop another franchisee who is encroaching, if necessary by rescinding his contract? If not, the territory agreement is of limited value.

8. STRINGS

The contract should specify what you have to buy from the franchisor and what you are free to buy from any other sources.

Franchisee note:

If a number of products are to be bought from the franchisor, is there a guarantee that they will be readily available at a fair price? Are you permitted to buy elsewhere if the franchisor cannot supply upon request, at the normal market price? Is a 'fair price' defined?

9. TRAINING

Is the length and content of training specified, including details of what costs the franchisee must bear? (It is common for franchisees to have to pay for hotel charges and travel to and from the training course).

Franchisee note:

Are the details of the programme specified - are the aims clearly laid out, so that at the end of the course you can judge if you have been properly trained? For example, if the aims state that at the end of course you will be able to understand and apply the basic rules of management accounting, and at the end you cannot, then you should be entitled to ask for extra training. Do not accept that it is your fault - unless you have missed the sessions, or fallen asleep in them following a bout of lunch-time drinking. The franchisor has vetted you and judged you to be suitable for the course.

If you are seeing this as a joint venture with your husband, wife, girlfriend or boyfriend, can that other person be trained too? (This should be specified in writing).

Is the training held at the right time? (I have come across franchises in which the training sessions are only held three times a year, so those who sign up at the wrong time and you find the training is offered three months after they open the shop. Not only is this three months too late, by that time you cannot possibly afford to go away for a week to undergo the training programme.)

Is the course held at a reasonable location? Most people expect to travel for training, but if you are in Aberdeen and the training is suddenly switched from Edinburgh to Penzance you may begin to wonder if it is all worth it.

10. SUPPORT

The franchisor should specify exactly what sort of support he is offering - is there a hot line for urgent enquiries, do you get to see a rep from head office once a month...

Franchisee note:

Beware of vague promises. In the early days you may well need urgent and immediate help, and if your calls for guidance and help are constantly be met with comments such as "I'll get someone to call you back..." it can be very frustrating.

11. LAUNCH ADVERTISING

The franchisor should give specific details of what will be done, how much it will cost, who will pay for it and who will arrange it, and what sort of response rate is expected.

Franchisee note:

Beware of anything spoken of in purely general terms such as "Our dynamic launch campaign will have customers queuing at the door from Day 1." Think now of what will happen if it does not.

12. OPERATIONS MANUAL

You can't see this until you sign the contract, but there should be clear indications that there is such a manual and of what it contains.

Franchisee note:

Some 15% of franchisees responding to questions asked by The Good Franchise Guide stated that their franchise either had no manual at all or that it simply did not cover important matters. If the promotional literature speaks of the manual telling you "everything you need to know" bear that in mind when questioning other franchisees.

13. DECOR
Many franchisors like all their franchisees' shops to look the same. That is fair enough and you can budget for the opening work.

Franchise note:
What happens if the franchisor decides to update the decor? Are you obliged to do a total refit at your own cost just because the franchisor says so? Is the franchisor obliged to give any warning? Is there a limit on how much you might be expected to spend?

14. SELLING PRICES
If there is a price-fixing agreement to stop one franchisee undercutting another this should be specified here.

Franchise note:
Are you agreeing to sell at a price fixed by the franchisor? If so what can you do if a rival firm (possibly another franchise) opens up next door and undercuts your price by 20%? Make sure that you really can sell at the price you are quoting to the market you are promised. If you are taking on a printing franchise and the franchisor suggests you ought to be able to sell to local businesses on the industrial estates, check just what they are paying for print. Do not expect it to be the same as the customer in the high street.

15. SELLING THE FRANCHISE
There will probably be a lot of restrictions on how the franchise may be disposed of if you wish to do so before the end of the agreement.

Franchisee note:
Are there any unreasonable restrictions on selling, such as the new owner paying special levies to the franchisor? Do you have to pay a close-down penalty?

Look out also for lease and loan penalties for early repayments or transfers to other people.

16. SALES LEVELS
Some franchise agreements actually stipulate that franchisees will reach certain sales levels each month. In other words you have to buy in x amount of stock whether you are selling it or not.

Franchisee note:

I strongly suggest you should take great care with such agreements, for they can represent a way of franchisors protecting themselves against a recession at the expense of their franchisees. Of course such clauses are always explained away as merely covering "extreme cases of inactivity on the part of a franchisee". The implication is that you, being a great salesman and natural for the role of franchisee will have no problem in reaching these figures.

Perhaps that is true. But what about seasonal trends? What about the time when you have appendicitis and your junior staff do well to keep the operation ticking over but really cannot be expected to keep up the normal sales levels? "We wouldn't dream of applying the clause in such circumstances," the franchisor might say. In which case why is the clause there in the first place? Remember you may be obliged to pay for compulsory monthly purchases through direct debit or standing orders, so you cannot even hold back payments if you run into trouble.

17. PAYMENT OF FEES

The contract should specify what needs to be paid to the franchisor and when it is to be paid.

Franchisee note:

Exactly when money is to be paid is a vital point in balancing cash flow. How will you pay this money if it is to be paid out before you start earning? Is there VAT to be paid? If so remember that it can take time before you get the VAT back from Customs and Excise.

18. TRADE SECRETS

It is not unreasonable for a franchisor to expect his franchisees to keep trade secrets and most contracts will have a clause to this effect.

Franchisee note:

What is a trade secret? Is the secrets clause stated in such a way that should you ever open a business of your own in the same field as the franchise you will be liable to the charge of misusing trade secrets? Beware particularly of clauses which relate to 'know-how'. This highly general term can be used to stop you doing anything!

This question is worth considering a little further with the following examples:

Mr White works as a franchisee for four years but at the end of that feels that a combination of the restrictions on what he is not allowed to sell, the royalty he has to pay on turnover and the cost of goods he has to buy from the franchisor all conspire against him making a decent return on his investment. He would, he feels, do better selling the franchise running the same sort of business on his own.

Mrs Green has run her franchise for four years with great success and is ready to expand. She and her husband consider buying a second franchise but then hit on the idea of Mr Green setting up a similar business to the one his wife already runs in a neighbouring town, but without buying into a franchise. After all, Mrs Green argues, they already know more about running that franchise than the franchisor and they have certainly learned all about stock control, purchasing, credit control and accounting.

Mr Black has had his franchise for four years and it has not been a great success. He wants to get out and turn the leasehold premises he currently uses into a totally new form of business.

Mr Brown has run the franchise for 15 years and the franchise agreement has now run out. Having learned all he needs to know he wants to run the same type of business on his own, without the back up of a franchisor. He knows he can take up a lease on premises a mile from those leased for the franchise, and has no doubt that he can quickly recruit new staff for his venture.

What is the franchisor's reaction to each of these perfectly commonplace situations? It will of course vary from case to case but watch out for any clause in the agreement that suggests that you or your immediate family must not set up in a directly competitive business within 50 miles or within 3 years of ceasing to be a franchisee. Given what the franchisor has invested in the network and the franchisee it may be thought that such restrictions are really not too unfair, but they show how the reality of signing a franchise contract can be with you even after the contract comes to an end.

The reason that three out of four people in our example wanted to set up without the franchisor was that they had learned the 'know-how', become successful and felt that there was not much else to the franchisor's business. This is indeed one of the great weaknesses of franchising. If the franchise does not have a name that is widely known among potential customers (who for example does not know the name Dyno Rod) and does not offer something which is unique and patented, then the franchise offers little other than know-how. Knowledge, when you do not have it, often seems mysterious and awe- inspiring. When you do have it, it can seem so obvious and simple that to find yourself restricted because of it can be rather galling and not a little frustrating.

19. STANDARDS WITHIN THE BUSINESS

Obviously the franchisee is obliged to maintain standards within the business he is operating and the franchisee will almost certainly be asked to agree to "maintain reasonable standards".

Franchisee note:

In what way are these standards to be measured? Talk to franchisees already operating this franchise in order to ascertain if the franchisor does use this clause to force franchisees to act in particular ways which may be considered by some to be unreasonable.

20. RECORD KEEPING

All businesses need to keep other records for their own well-being and for the taxation authorities. Franchisees need records in addition to ensure that the correct royalty payments are made and to give feed- back to the franchisor on how things are going. The contract should lay down what the franchisor can legitimately ask for. It will also normally state that the franchisor should be given access to the books at reasonable times in order to check the figures.

Franchisee note:

Check to see if any other records are required, and discover from franchisees how much time this might take up.

21. SPECIAL EVENTUALITIES

Franchisors can create new lines, new promotional ideas, and new add-ons to the franchised business. Many of these developments can be very exciting indeed, offering ever greater chances for additional profits. The contract will probably allow the franchisor to introduce such new lines and require the franchisees to sell them.

Franchisee note:

It is often the case that the introduction of such new lines involves the franchisee in additional expenditure through development of the premises and the buying in of new equipment. You should be aware of just how much power the franchisor has to enforce such developments upon you. Always remember, if your royalty is based on turnover, then it can be in the franchisor's interests to continue to think up new lines since they will invariably increase turnover long before they increase profit and they can be disastrous for your cash flow.

22. STAFFING

The franchisor will require the franchisee to employ sufficient staff trained to the right standard to maintain the business in a proper fashion.

Franchisee note:

As already noted, in many parts of the country finding staff is no problem. Elsewhere, despite apparently large numbers of unemployed, it is not unknown for businesses to be constantly short of staff. Even when vacancies are advertised under youth training and employment training schemes there may not be a single taker. This is obviously very frustrating for a franchisee who may have to do extra work himself in order to cope with the staff shortage. But it can lead to even greater problems if you have a contract which specifies that you have to have a certain number of staff. If pressured from this side you may end up offering jobs at far higher salaries than you should just to keep your franchisor happy.

Be careful also of clauses that can require you to send staff for training. Many businesses find that they have to use staff who they know will only be with them for short periods before moving onto another job. In such cases it may be ludicrous to train these employees in anything but the basics; make sure the contract does not insist that you do.

23. INSURANCE AND INDEMNITY

The contract will specify that the franchisee runs a separate business from the franchisor, and is not the franchisor's agent in the legal sense of the word.

Franchisee note:

What this means in practice is that the franchisor cannot be held responsible for any problems the franchisee creates.

The agreement will normally specify this, which means that the obligation is on the franchisee to take out all the necessary insurance to cover any eventuality. You will need insurance cover on the building (whether you own it or not), on the contents within the building, on any vehicles, and on public liability.

24. FORCE MAJEURE

Virtually all agreements tend to have a force majeure clause which effectively wipes out most of the agreement in the case of national emergencies.

Franchisee note:

If you live and work in Northern Ireland it is worth gaining clarification of this clause as it relates to your circumstances. It is also worth ensuring that the clause really does allow both sides to escape from obligations. If you operate a franchise selling imported goods and there is a national dock strike then clearly your franchisor will not be able to get stock to you, and will need to be cleared of his obligations during the strike.

Likewise you will not be able to meet your obligations to achieve a certain level of turnover, and you need to be absolved from your obligations both during and for some time after the strike.

25. CHANGE OF FRANCHISOR

The contract should assure franchisees that it cannot be breached either by the franchisee or franchisor. Further if the franchisor sells out and a new company takes its place the contract should be continued. Remember also the clauses that stop you operating in competition and taking know-how with you if you opt out.

CHAPTER 9

HOW COULD IT POSSIBLY FAIL?

One of the central themes of this book is that although taking on a recognised franchise dramatically reduces your chances of finding yourself involved in a business failure, it is not a guarantee against failure.

While no one likes to think of failure, lessons can be learned (before it is too late) by considering why some franchises do fail and keeping a constant look-out for any signs that these problems may fall upon you once you have started operating.

The box on the next page summarises of some of the reasons why franchises fail. This chapter looks at these ideas in more detail. As you move towards a decision on the franchise you want to take on, refer back to the box and ask yourself: could it happen to me?

- Initial advertising does not work - no customers
- Another firm (possibly franchised by a rival outfit) sets up doing the same thing next door
- The franchisor increases the royalty rates
- The franchisor goes into liquidation
- The franchisor orders a total refit to match new image of the company - at your expense
- Sales are so low you are verging on bankruptcy - perhaps because of variation from one part of the country to another
- Your personal circumstances change and you can no longer have the support or your husband/wife
- You turn out to be the wrong sort of person to run a franchise after all

There are two basic causes of franchise failure - the failure of the franchisor to maintain the whole operation and look after the franchisees, and the failure of the franchisee to run his own business properly.

IF THE FRANCHISOR LIQUIDATES

If a franchisor liquidates, the franchisees do not lose their businesses, since each franchised business is a separate legal entity.

However, what the sudden demise of a franchisor does mean is that the franchisee's back-up and support suddenly disappears. Any national advertising the franchisee may have had will vanish - the regular supply of goods will likewise cease and the franchisees will quickly have to seek out their own suppliers on the best terms they can get.

How much this affects each franchisee depends on the nature of the franchise, but it is certainly worth considering from the very start what you would do if the franchisor failed. If you are selling one particular line of goods all of which are supplied by the franchisor, you may immediately be in serious trouble - although there are always ways out. Together with other franchisees you will have a fair amount of buying power, which in turn means that you will be able to go to other suppliers and offer to become outlets for their products instead, providing the price is right.

Indeed it is not unknown for franchisees to wish actively that their franchisor would go down, so that they could start out on their own without having to pay any royalties and without having to buy in items only from the franchisor. But the reality for those franchisees who have suffered in this way tends to suggest that the disappearance of the franchisor can be more traumatic than might be imagined.

One sure way to increase your chances of survival even if the franchisor liquidates soon after you have become a franchisee is to stay in touch with other franchisees who are willing to help you out as they solve their own problems. Obviously no franchisee is going to place your interests in front of his own, but people do have bonds that bring them together when disaster strikes. Certainly if you have cemented friendships in happier days you are likely to benefit later.

All of which leaves just one situation for which there is virtually no solution: when you are one of the first franchisees to take up a franchise. Our advice here is that under normal circumstances you should not be one of the first to take up a franchise unless all the following conditions are fulfilled:

There are at least two tried and tested pilot schemes still in operation which you can visit and verify

You are quite sure of the bona fides of the franchisor

You are paying little or nothing by way of an up-front franchise fee. If you are unable to negotiate a zero franchise fee in view of the fact that this is a starting point for the franchise you should at least get the fee payable in stages spread over the first 18 months that you are trading

You feel that you have enough experience and background in this line of business to make it work without the franchisor

Whatever else you do, remember that handing over a fee to a franchisor is an unsecured investment. If the company has no assets you are unlikely to get anything back if things go wrong.

IF THE FRANCHISEE FAILS

Franchisees fail for any one of six reasons:

1. Arrogance.
The arrogant franchisee has seen it all before, done it all before, and knows that he knows better than anyone else. On the training course he tells the other trainees that the real world isn't as painted by the tutors, and that by rights he ought to be up there giving the sessions. When setting up the business he ignores the manual, refusing to "waste" money on advertising campaigns he "knows" will not work. Listening to no one he blunders from crisis to crisis and eventually fails.

2. Directoritis.

The sufferer from directoritis knows what being the managing director of a company is all about. He put a sign saying "Managing Director" on the door of his office, gets a leather chair and a bigger desk and joins a couple of directors' clubs. He turns up late, takes a long lunch and leaves early speaking vaguely of "entertaining a customer". What he fails to notice is that the rest of the firm follow his example and the company quickly falls to pieces.

3. Debt-fear.

All companies start by making losses - the mere fact that you have to buy stock before you can sell it means you run a deficit. The franchisee with debt-fear is told countless times that the business will make a loss before it can make a profit but suddenly finds he cannot face the reality. He lies awake at night murmuring about "all that money I owe", and no attempt at logical reasoning concerning the balance sheet, long term prospects or investment for the future will have any effect. He quits.

4. Self-employment fear.

The cold reality of the end of the monthly pay cheque, the responsibility for the salaries of others, and the leasing agreements leads to panic for those that suffer from self- employment fear. Unlike most of the other problems this one strikes almost everyone who moves directly from employment to self-employment, although in most people it is quickly pushed to the back of the mind as the work begins to take over. Only when it remains after the first few days does it become a debilitating problem.

5. The eternal employee.

The eternal employee goes through the self- employment panic, and comes out with a view of the world which allows him to believe he is still cocooned in the safe world of employment. He does this by believing that despite all that is said to the contrary the franchisor is his boss. If something goes wrong the franchisor will sort it out; the franchisor will tell him what to do, and bail out any losses. When this does not happen the business collapses.

6. Family fiends.

Family fiends tell each other and their friends what pressure that franchisee is under, and how everyone is taking advantage of the franchisee. The franchisor is exploiting him with the demands for the royalty payment. Suppliers are demanding too much for poor quality goods. Staff are expecting too many perks and privileges. Inevitably staff leave, suppliers stop supplying and the franchisor does not bother to call and find out if all is in order, since all they get back is a mouthful of complaints.

But do not start to believe that franchising is all bad news. Each year the GOOD FRANCHISE GUIDE questions hundreds of franchisees about their work and the picture that emerges is remarkably consistent.

Around 85% of franchisees who reply to the publication's questionnaires state that they are doing as well as, or better than expected. These franchisees do have complaints of course, but the overwhelming majority of these relate to how hard the work is.

As for the 15% who are doing worse than they expected (that is they are not meeting the franchisor's predictions in terms of profit) there is no simple explanation that emerges from the research that explains why they are doing badly. The responses from this failing group have been analysed geographically, in relation to the time the franchisor has been in operation, the background of the franchisees in question, and a range of other factors. None of them shows a consistent relationship with the fact of failure.

In a few cases the reasons are clearly laid down by the franchisees - and mostly these relate to inadequacies of the geographic area. But these explanations (which may of course be little more than excuses) relate to no more than a handful of franchisees.

To find a fuller explanation it is necessary to read through the commentaries written by franchisees for THE GOOD FRANCHISE GUIDE and to talk with franchisees who are experiencing difficulties. From this one gets a picture of three major reasons for failure:

1. Inability or lack of willingness to improvise when the franchise does not appear to be developing. For example, if the initial promotion does not bring in much in the way of work, not thinking carefully of the reasons for the failure, talking to other franchisees, and then undertaking a revised scheme of advertising using your own initiative - and money.
2. Unwillingness to work very, very hard indeed. In this context very, very hard can mean from 5.30am to midnight seven days a week in the early stages.

3. Lack of customer friendliness. Over and over again franchisees complain about the way the public treat them - there is almost a consensus that the Great British Public now treat anyone in business as a crook and as fair game for abuse, unwarranted complaints, failure to pay and so on. In the face of this, the new businessman has both to make money and stay user-friendly. It appears that some personality types simply cannot cope with this.

In considering these three reasons for failure it should be remembered that the research that reveals these is based on franchisees whose names and addresses are willingly given to the GOOD FRANCHISE GUIDE by franchisors. In other words a franchisor who knows he has a very high rate of failure among his franchisees is unlikely to give their names and addresses to a publication like the GUIDE. When we recognise that half the franchisors in the UK do refuse to give names and addresses, it shows once more just how careful you have to be in selecting the right franchise for you.

Whatever the reason for the failure of a franchise, franchisees who find themselves in this position have to consider what to do next.

There are two courses of action - to sell the business in the market- place as a going concern, or to sell it back the franchisor. Some franchise agreements have a clear commitment that the first refusal must be offered to the franchisor. This may sound encouraging but it does not mean that the franchisor will take over the franchise - it just means he has the option to buy at what may be a very low price.

WHAT CAN BE SOLD

If a franchisee does fail we can now consider what is now available for sale.

Firstly there is the actual franchise - that is the right to operate the franchise. The franchisor will have to be involved in any sale of this right of operation since he will need to ensure that the franchise contract commitments are still met. How much this is worth is a matter for negotiation. On the one hand anyone wishing to take up a new franchise will have to pay the full franchise fee, find premises and so on - this is all done in one go. Against this the franchisee will have to explain why he is pulling out - after all it is not much of an advertisement to say "I've failed to make it work, but I'll sell it to you for a fat fee."

Secondly the equipment you have bought. Presumably this is as specified by the franchisor, and so will be required by any new franchisee.

Finally the leases on buildings, vehicles, equipment etc. You have to keep paying these leases until someone comes along and takes them off your hands. Again the franchisor or a new franchisee ought to be interested in taking such items.

If not, however, you have a financial commitment which may be hard to get out of.

In summary, if the franchise fails and you wish to cease trading it is often difficult merely to say "I'll write off my franchise fee as a loss and call it a day," because of the cost of leased items. All in all you are better off staying on reasonable terms with the franchisor and trying to sell everything back to him, even if it is at a knockdown price. The more you argue with the franchisor and accuse him of being at fault if your franchise fails the less likely you are to be able to enlist his help if you wish to assign leases.

CHAPTER 10

WHICH FRANCHISES ARE AVAILABLE?

This publication concludes with details of some of the franchises currently on the market having a total investment cost of £50,000 or less.

There are more franchises available than those listed here - and of course many new ones coming onto the market all the time. You will find references to such franchises in the Daily Mail itself, and in the many magazines that now exist which carry articles on franchising. You will also find a number of reference books on the market, each of which naturally makes some particular claim to being the best. One may claim to be definitive, another to be "prize winning" another may see itself as "Directory of the Year" and so on. You may wonder why in the relatively small field of franchised businesses there should be so many directories.

I would not try to hide the fact that on the question of franchise directories I am biased, being the editor of one of them: THE GOOD FRANCHISE GUIDE. Therefore in what follows you should bear in mind the fact that many other commentators on franchising will not agree with my comments.

The vast majority of listings books for franchises are put together by people with a vested interest in franchising. For the most part the publishers of such texts are themselves agents (or, as they are often known, 'consultants') who have the job of finding suitable franchisees for their clients. This means that the comments that appear in their books and magazines are not likely to be unbiased. Worse, such publications can, in extreme cases, be used to fly franchising kites.

Where the consultant hears of a possible franchise he offers to list it in his franchise magazine or directory free of charge. If the would-be franchisor then receives a suitably large number of calls from would-be franchisees he or she may feel that there is a market out there for this type of franchise. If on the other hand there are few calls the franchise is quietly withdrawn. This explains the disappearance of over one hundred franchises a year from the combined totals of these sponsored directories. Put another way, 20% of franchisees supposedly on offer this year will have vanished completely within the next twelve months.

To avoid being caught by this sort of trick you should try and use more than one reference book when searching for the right franchisor for you (since rival consultants will not do each other's franchises a favour by giving them full and fair listings),and to try and use at least one reference book that very clearly does not have a link with any outside organisation.

My criticism of franchise consultants who publish directories does not imply there is something wrong with the concept of franchise consultants as such. It is perfectly reasonable for a firm with expertise at running its own business to call in consultants when considering a totally new way of operating a business. Seeking out the right franchisee is also a specialist task and again it is reasonable to seek guidance. But there are franchise consultants whose activities ARE less desirable than they might be, and it is worth treading with some caution in this area.

This problem has arisen in part because of the intense rivalry between consultants. This in turn has led to a great increase in the level of secrecy surrounding individual franchises, with franchisors under instruction from consultants not to supply more than the most basic details of the franchise until the would-be franchisee has been vetted by the consultant. Likewise the highly dubious habit has grown up of franchisors refusing to supply names and addresses of existing franchisees to enquirers. This in itself is most odd since all franchisees must have publicity if they are to survive in the market- place. None of the franchisors that I have contacted who have this policy of secrecy have ever offered any explanation except to hide behind the catch-all phrase of secrecy being "company policy". Such secrecy is completely against the BFA code of practice and in my opinion says nothing positive about the companies that indulge in it.

As you review each franchise elsewhere, refer back to this chapter and check your findings against the preliminary tests outlined below. If you have any doubts then be cautious - there is going to be an awful lot of money at stake.

We have already talked about the way a franchise deals with you when you make your first enquiry. If you are not impressed by your opening request for information, then look elsewhere, for first impressions are often very important in selecting a business partner. While you may choose not to exclude any particular franchisor immediately, you should take extra caution with any franchise that

a) fails to respond to your request for information first time around

b) responds in a very hard sell fashion, phoning or visiting without first sending you the details you have requested

c) supplies poorly produced material, especially when provided without a phone number or full address.

d) supplies material which does not answer basic questions about costs, training and expected profit.

Having selected a franchise that passes your preliminary tests, you should next consider each of the following points. In each case, an example of dubious practices which you might care to be wary of is given:

1. Is the concept a distributorship dressed up as a franchise?

Universal Metals Ltd manufacture a wide range of tools and spares for popular cars. The range is sold through car dealers, garages, second-hand car sales rooms, motor factors (wholesalers) and the like. In all there are about 45,000 such locations in the UK and head office of Universal Metals is finding it expensive to maintain a team of salesmen who can visit each potential outlet regularly.

One day a bright young executive at Universal decides that Universal Metals will offer franchises. The franchisee pays a fee (say £7000) for the privilege of becoming a franchisee, and also pays to lease and equip a van in which he can tour the countryside visiting garages and the like. The franchisee needs to keep his van fully topped up with Universal products and of course these must be paid for. This means money for Universal from the very start. The franchisee then sets off visiting garages and selling Universal products at suitable discounts. In other words the franchisee does exactly what the travelling salesman did, but has to pay for the right to do it.

The benefits for Universal are enormous - they no longer have to pay any salesmen; their new salesmen (their franchisees) pay Universal. They no longer need to equip any vans, (the franchisee does this at his own expense) and no longer need to worry about motivating the sales force (the franchisee has to work incredibly hard because it is his money that is invested).

There are many variations on this theme, and it would be quite unjust to suggest that you should avoid all of them. But the message here is that if you look at a franchise which has any of the following points think hard about the implications.

- Does the franchisee just deal in the products of one manufacturer?
- Does the franchisee act as a salesman for one manufacturer?
- Does the franchisee have to pay the manufacturer for all his stock before he sells it on?

If the answer is always yes, ask yourself, might you not be better off as a travelling salesman?

2. Does the franchise really give you any trade advantages?

Megavan Carriers offer a next-day delivery service around the UK. Any business can phone up the nearest depot of Megavan and ask for a van to arrive that evening and pick up parcels which will be delivered the following day. Companies which have regular consignments can arrange a regular service in which a van will automatically turn up every night and take whatever parcels are ready. The sending company pays a standard fee for each parcel sent.

A new scheme is then developed: Megavan depots around the country will be set up and run by franchisees. Each franchisee should already have premises on an industrial estate near other firms that are likely to want to send out parcels. The franchisee pays a franchise fee (say £5000) plus the same amount again for industrial scales and other equipment. He then tells all the neighbouring firms that if anyone has any parcels they should drop them round by 4pm for guaranteed next day delivery. He quotes the standard price per parcel knowing that for each parcel sent he will receive a £1.00 commission from Megavan.

This all seems straightforward until one realises that in the transport business all prices are negotiable. We have already noted that Megavan will turn up anywhere to collect parcels on a daily basis, not just at the franchisees address. There is clearly nothing to stop anyone (franchised or not) sending a circular round to other firms saying "We have a daily collection service - if you want anything transmitted by a next day service just drop it in to us". Then as the volume of goods despatched goes up better prices can be negotiated, leaving an ever wider gap between the price being charged to neighbouring factories and the price being paid to the courier.

In other words, the 5000 franchise fee and 5000 set up costs were all wasted. There was no need for the franchisee to take up a franchise since he could have done exactly the same work, and made the same amount of money (if not more) using the same courier, but acting as an individual.

Points For Reflection
- Could I possibly set up this business on my own?
- Does being a franchisee of this firm give me any real advantages?
- How would this firm deal with me if I was a large buyer of their goods or services rather than a franchisee?

Remember, setting up as a franchisee is expensive, and may tie you into one supplier. Make sure you are getting your money's worth.

3. What makes this franchise special?

Astonishingly Fast Printers want to offer you the right to run their franchise in Yourtown. Included in the deal is the guarantee that no other branch of Astonishingly will open within 30 miles of you.

Astonishingly FP branches cover most of the country, and you are lucky that in Yourtown there is not one already. It sounds like a great opportunity.

But now ask yourself, why should anyone choose to use Astonishingly FP where there are already half a dozen instant printers dotted around Yourtown, all of which are famous names in the high street quick printing business?

You may be told that Astonishingly FP is recognised by people as the best, the fastest, the most reliable in the business. Are such claims really true? You may be told that Astonishingly FP is the biggest fast print business in the country. Does that matter?

In other words, when a businessman needs some printing done does he really seek out the nearest branch of Astonishingly FP Fast Printers? Or does he pop into the nearest or most convenient instant print shop on the basis that they are all much of a muchness. The franchisor might tell you that instant printers are not all the same, and to someone in the trade that might be obvious. But what matters is the perception of the man in the street. The guarantee of exclusive territory is not worth much if there are several firms (franchised or otherwise) all offering a service which is perceived by the public as being virtually identical, for even if these rival franchises are not already trading in your area, they soon might be. Could your new franchise really take the strain of a business opening up next door which differs in little more than name only?

- Does outside competition matter?
- If there is little or no competition at present, is it possible that competition will suddenly spring up? Will that affect you?

4. The product is so new that no one has heard of it yet.

Special consideration must be given to any unique service or product which is not universally known. It is always exciting to hear of a new idea that will soon "revolutionize" the market place, and even more exciting to be in on the ground floor as the idea is about to start. After all, most of the people we hear of who have accumulated vast wealth appear to have done it by being in at the start of some new venture or enterprise.

But there is a problem as we have seen for new franchises can fail, just as easily as any other new type of business. Unless you are an inveterate gambler with a small fortune to risk, stay away from new franchises until you can see clear evidence that they have proven their worth. Such evidence should come in the form of working pilot schemes, with full audited accounts which are quite separate from the main accounts of the franchisor, along with open access to the pilot operation on a day-to-day basis. The charges made to the franchisee should also be lower than you might otherwise expect in recognition of the newness of the scheme.

- Does this franchise offer something unique, or if not, does it offer a name that is so well known that the public seek out that name, even though there are rivals which may be cheaper and more convenient?

5. The franchise works throughout the country so there is no doubt it will work in Yourtown.

Assuming the franchise has worked elsewhere, is there any difference in your area? Some franchises simply don't replicate easily to all parts of the country, and you should investigate any noticeable gaps in the network.

> • Are there any special requirements for the franchise, such as a large number of private cars in the area, high disposable incomes, large number of hotels in the vicinity etc?

6. The franchisor who takes care of all the buying so that you don't have to worry about locating any supplies.

Of course that sounds utterly wonderful, but it can become a source of discontent if you find yourself tied to paying high prices for goods that are not always available.

> • How closely will you be tied to the franchisor? Do you have to buy everything from him, or do you have flexibility and freedom?

7. The product that sells itself

No matter how wonderful a product or service it will need advertising in order to bring it to the attention of the public. Advertising is a specialist trade and it is not unreasonable to assume that the franchisor has spent some considerable time working on the advertising necessary for the franchise, and now has a clear idea of how to do it and how to get it right.

> • How good is the national and local advertising? Do you see any national advertising?

8. The franchisor who is so anxious to have you he doesn't even ask any questions.

Franchisors ought to be as cautious of you as you are of them. There are after all a large number of people around who should not be franchisees.

- Does the franchisor ask you a lot of questions? Does he care about you in a way that makes you think he cares about his franchise? If he doesn't seem to worry about how you will get on, you might begin to wonder.

APPROACHING A FRANCHISOR: WHAT TO LOOK OUT FOR

- Is it a distributorship in disguise?
- Is it possible to set up without paying franchise fees simply by becoming a customer of the franchisor?
- Does the franchise offer something unique?
- If the service or product is not unique is it so well known and so popular that people will use the service or buy the product despite alternatives being available?
- If the franchise is new and untried is there a good pilot scheme available which you can examine in detail?

At this stage one very helpful activity for the would-be franchisee is to contact the British Franchise Association and order a copy of their Franchisee Information Pack. This contains the very latest list of franchises which are on the market along with two very helpful booklets - "The Ethics of Franchising" and "How to Evaluate a Franchise" which you should read.

The title "The Ethics of Franchising" is not one that will excite most potential franchisees, but you should persevere for this book spells out what you should expect from the franchisor. If a franchisor tells you that what you are asking for is "not normal in franchising" and the Ethics book tells you otherwise then you should rapidly move on to another franchise.

Now it is up to you. Being a franchisee is a very good way of setting up and running your own business if you are willing to learn, follow directions and work hard. If you feel your personality fits the bill, make sure that you now select a reputable and well-known franchisor. Good luck, and I look forward to talking to you when I conduct my next survey of franchisees.

LIST OF FRANCHISES

The following is a selective list of franchisors who are known to have franchises available at a total cost of approximately £50,000 and below, but should in no sense be regarded as a recomendation, from the Daily Mail, the publishers of this book or the author, of the franchises included.

NUMBER OF OUTLETS
This includes both franchisor owned and franchisee owned outlets. In most cases the franchisor may retain ownership of just one or two locations, but there are exceptions, especially where a company has moved into franchising after having set up its own dealer network. Extra care should be taken when dealing with a franchisor who has a short history, or a very limited number of franchisees.

SET UP COSTS
This figure includes the franchise fee plus all capital outlay on equipment and the like, but excludes items which may be leased. It does not normally include any provision for the losses which all new franchises inevitably make during the opening months.

The fact that leasing agreements are excluded should not be allowed to hide the fact that a lease is a legal commitment to pay a fixed sum of money per month.

The set up costs shown here do not include VAT, which normally has to be paid on all items required at the start of the franchise. VAT paid at the launch of a business is usually recoverable eventually from Customs and Excise, but there may be a delay in getting it back.

ROYALTIES
Most franchises offer a straightforward fixed royalty but some do have additional royalties for national advertising, while others vary their royalty depending on length of time the franchise has been in operation, and its

level of turnover. A few franchises charge the royalty only on specific elements of the turnover, or alternatively vary the rate depending on the origin of the income. The figure shown is that paid by most franchisees including any additional royalties.

BFA MEMBERSHIP

The British Franchise Association is recognised as the major association representing franchisors in the UK. Although membership is generally considered to be a sign of a well-established and well-run franchise it must be remembered that BFA membership is neither a guarantee of success nor of automatic profits. Full membership requires evidence of a correctly constituted pilot scheme successfully operated for at least one year, financed and managed by the applicant company. In addition, evidence of successful franchising over a subsequent two-year period with at least four franchisees is required. Associate membership requires proof of a correctly constituted pilot scheme successfully operated for at least one year, financed and managed by the applicant company and with evidence of successful franchising for a period of one year with at least one franchisee.

A1 Damproofing

New Side Mill, Charnley Fold Lane, Bamber Bridge,
Preston, Lancs PR5 6AA
Phone: 0772 35228

Damproofing and treatment of woodworm, wood rot, rising damp and condensation using a chemical which the franchisor manufactures. Launched in 1985 the franchise is growing at around 5 franchisees a year.

Number of outlets	35
Set up costs	£24000
Royalties payable	10.0%
BFA Membership?	Yes

Add-Itt Intro Franchising

Franchise House, Kelham Street Industrial Estate,
Doncaster, South Yorks. DN1 3QU
Phone: 0302 320269
Retail of car care additives and maintenance products plus own branding
of automotive chemicals and aerosols. The sale of the franchisor's own
brands is central to the operation - hence the lack of royalties.

Number of outlets	18
Set up costs	£10,000
Royalties payable	No royalties payable

Al Fullers International Rent-a-Car

230 Burlington road, New Malden, Surrey KT3 4NO
Phone: 01-949 8122
Car and van rental - one of a growing number of rivals to the established
force of Hertz, Budget and the like.

Number of outlets	12
Set up costs	£16655
Royalties payable	7.5%
BFA membership?	No

Alan Paul PLC

Alan Paul House, 164 New Chester Road, Birkenhead,
Merseyside L41 9BG
Phone: 051-666 1060
Hairdressing salon, from the same franchisor as the Body and Face Place.
While competition is heavy this franchisor is in the BFA, which sets it
aside from several others.

Number of outlets	39
Set up costs	£40,000
Royalties payable	10%
BFA membership?	Yes

Alarms Direct PLC

EBC House, Kew Road, Richmond,
Surrey TW9 2NA
Phone: 01-332 1056
Home security franchise offering "the best security system on the market" (according to the franchisor). Currently offering up to ten franchises a year.

Number of outlets	6
Set up costs	£15000
Royalties payable	None
BFA membership?	No

Alpine Soft Drinks (UK) Ltd

Richmond Way, Chelmsley Wood,
Birmingham B37 7TT
Phone: 021-770 6816
Manufacturer of soft drinks using Alpine, Big Apple and Drifter trade names. These are sold via door to door delivery services.

Number of outlets	230
Set up costs	£7000
Royalties payable	10%
BFA membership?	Yes

Alphagraphics Printshops of The Future

Ryedale Building, 58/60 Piccadilly, York, YO1 1NX
Tel: 0904 611344
The new generation of worldwide electronic printshops, extensive copying, printing and binding facilities, with "Lazergraphics" computerised design and typesetting, incorporating the unique "Alphalink" international electronic document transmission system.

Number of outlets	17
Set up costs	£160,000
Royalties payable	8% decreasing to 3%
BFA membership?	Yes

Amberchem Systems Ltd

7 Waymills Industrial Estate, Whitchurch, Shropshire, SY13 1RT
Phone: 0948-6234
A mobile vehicle based franchise selling a large range of chemical products to direct to the builder. Allows the franchise to develop profitably with everything you need to make selling a success from day one.

Number of outlets	2
Set up costs	£3,500
Royalties payable	5% Gross Sales
BFA membership?	Applied For

Ashfield Personnel

Ashfield Franchising, 21 Bridge Street,
Hemel Hempstead, Herts HP1 1EG
Phone: 0442 216618
Recently formed employment Agency - pilot launched in 1988.

Number of outlets	5
Set up costs	£35,000
Royalties payable	9.5%
BFA membership?	No

ATZ Business Consultants Ltd

Berkeley Square House, Berkeley Square, London W1X 6AE
Phone: 01-409 7000
Management and business consultancy founded by group of business people who have run their own companies. Plans to have over 200 franchises eventually.

Number of outlets	34
Set up costs	£15,000
Royalties payable	20%
BFA membership?	No

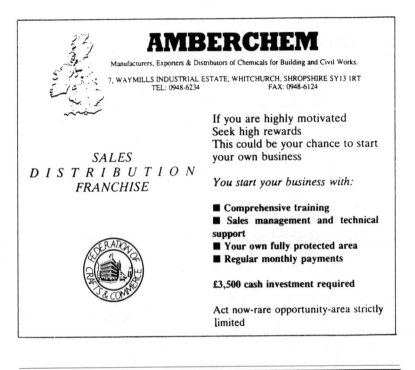
Autosheen Car Valeting Services Ltd

Unit 4 Everitt Close, Denington Industrial Estate,
Wellingborough, Kettering NN8 2QE
Phone: 0933 410047
Car valeting franchise which claims to be the "market leader"

Number of outlets	120
Set up costs	£8,950
Royalties payable	12.5% and £270 per month
BFA membership?	Associate

Banson Tool Hire

Pellon Lane, Halifax, West Yorkshire HX1 5SB
Phone: 0422 331177
Hire and sale of equipment for builders and DIY users such as picks and shovels. Clients also include local authorities. The brochure was particularly commended by the Good Franchise Guide.

Number of outlets	16
Set up costs	£50,000
Royalties payable	15%
BFA membership?	Associate

Baskin - Robbins Intenational Co Ltd

Glacier House, Oldfield Lane, Greenford, Middx,
Tel: 01- 575 2004
Said to be the worlds largest franchised ice-cream operation. Ice-cream stores offering 31 flavours of ice cream, sundaes, shakes, specials, sodas, and speciality Baskin-Robbins party or desert ice cream cakes.

Number of outlets	45
Set up costs	£50,000
Royalties payable	None
BFA membership?	No

The Bath Doctor

Britannia House, Leagrave Road, Luton, Beds
Phone: 0582 459336
Bathroom suite resurfacing. Started in 1982 and expanding steadily but in a competitive market.

Number of outlets	40
Set up costs	£16000
Royalties payable	12.5%
BFA membership?	Yes

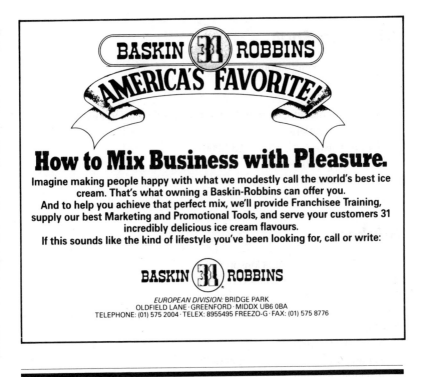
Bellina Ltd

31 Knightsdale Road, Ipswich, Suffolk IP1 4JJ
Phone: 0473 47444
Operator of a range of specialist chocolate shops retailing their own brand of hand made Belgian sweets. Lack of preservatives within the chocolates is an added selling point.

Number of outlets	9
Set up costs	£28,000
Royalties payable	None
BFA membership?	Associate

The Blind Spot

20A Park Road, Peterborough,
Cambs PE1 2TD
Phone: 0733 312913
Window blind manufacturer and retail franchise launched in 1988.

Number of outlets	2
Set up costs	£32,000
Royalties payable	7%
BFA membership?	No

Blinkers

Blinkers Franchising Ltd., Consort Court,
High Street, Fareham, Hants PO16 7AN
Phone: 0329 2330580
Hairdressing salon franchise launched in 1986 but growing quite slowly thus far.

Number of outlets	5
Set up costs	£30,000
Royalties payable	12%
BFA membership?	Associate

Bow Belles Bridal Hire Ltd

Brunswick Suite, Colwick Hall, Colwick Park,
Nottingham NG2 4BH
Phone: 0602 483317
Hire and sale of bridal wear, bridesmaid dresses and the like, run by ladies from their own homes.

Number of outlets	21
Set up costs	£15,000
Royalties payable	None
BFA membership?	No

Bruce and Company

43 Bridge Street, Leatherhead,
Surrey KT22 8BN
Phone: 0372 375161
Estate agency selling businesses and financial services and offering a wide
range of financial services such as loans, pensions and so forth.

Number of outlets	16
Set up costs	£14,000
Royalties payable	5%
BFA membership?	No

Budget Rent A Car Int Inc

41 Marlowes, Hemel Hempstead,
Herts HP1 1LD
Phone: 0442 232555
Car, van and truck rental specialising in relatively new vehicles from one
of the market leaders, currently with over 100 franchisees in the UK.

Number of outlets	135
Set up costs	£20,000
Royalties payable	10%
BFA membership?	Yes

Building Preservation

40 Lune Street, Preston, Lancs
Phone: 0772 204007
A franchise in the field of dampness and timber decay which places great
emphasis on its research work. Looking for rapid expansion from its
present 9 franchisees.

Number of outlets	9
Set up costs	£11,000
Royalties payable	10%
BFA membership?	Applied

Cafe Marseilles,

The Coach House, South Road, Clifton, Rugby
Phone: 0788 535750
Supplies coffee making machines and coffee and related products to business premises. A highly competitive field which takes its profit from a mark up on the consumables.

Number of outlets	6
Set up costs	£14,000
Royalties payable	None
BFA membership?	No

Captain Cargo Ltd

Wetherby Road, Ascot Drive Industrial Estate,
Derby CE2 8HL
Phone: 0332 290810
Next day courier service.

Number of outlets	75
Set up costs	£16,000
Royalties payable	£20 per month
BFA membership?	No

Car Brokers (UK)

Cheapside Chambers, Cheapside, Bradford, West Yorkshire BD1 4HP
Phone: 0274 370512
Company launched in 1988 offering all the various ways of obtaining a vehicle - including buying, leasing, hiring, plus servicing when required.

Number of outlets	1
Set up costs	£1250
Royalties payable	1%
BFA membership?	No

- Carpetlink is a retail carpet franchise selling and fitting carpets in the mid-to-upper-quality ranges.
- The shops do not carry stock, which avoids the franchisee having to tie-up capital.
- Sales are generated from large-sized samples of a huge range of different patterns, colours and types of carpet.
- Orders are placed directly with manufacturers or wholesalers.
- Carpetlink believes that its system offers advantages to the customer over the large carpet retailing multiples in both choice and speed of delivery.
- Carpetlink provides full training and a turnkey business in which the franchisee receives a fully-equipped showroom with carpet samples, carpet display lecterns, etc.

Total investment, including working capital: £50,000.
Contact: David Norris or Graham Finch

For Superior Service

Carpetlink Ltd., 2a Pepper Street, Chester CH1 1DF
Telephone: (0244) 312687 Fax: (0244)317224

Carpet Link Ltd

2A Pepper Sreet, Chester, CH1 IO3
Phone: 0224 312687
Carpet retail showroom, selling carpets in mid to upper quality bracket, no stock as carpets sold from samples. Full months training provided, Franchise fee is for a full turnkey business with trading accounts open.

Number of outlets	2
Set up costs	£40000 - £60000
Royalties payable	6%
BFA membership?	Early
Development Category	

Chem-Dry Southern Services

1 York Road, St Albans, Herts AL1 4PL
Phone: 0727 40370
Carpet cleaning service using franchisor's own non-toxic cleaning system

Number of outlets	32
Set up costs	£9,000
Royalties payable	£80 to
	£110 per month
BFA membership?	No

Circles

Modernideas Ltd, 786 London Road, Larkfield, Maidstone, Kent
Phone: 0732 848966
Recently launched mobile video supply firm which will be of interest to those seeking to avoid taking on any staff.

Number of outlets	5
Set up costs	£23,000
Royalties payable	11.5%
BFA membership?	No

The Clean Team

Allans Estates Ltd, 2 Dain Street, Burslem,
Stoke on Trent ST6 3LN
Phone: 0782 575142
Office and domestic cleaning franchise which at present is being rather secretive about its activities - but may be more open once more franchisees are established.

Number of outlets	3
Set up costs	£9300
Royalties payable	12.5%
BFA membership?	No

Clothesline

158-162 Dumbarton Road, Glasgow G11 6XE
Phone: 041-339 0370
Discount fashion retail outlets originally selling ladies clothes but more recently adding a men's range. Totally Scottish based at present.

Number of outlets	14
Set up costs	£23,000
Royalties payable	None
BFA membership?	Associate

Coffeeman Management Ltd

73 Woolsbridge Industrial Park, Wimborne, Dorset BH21 6SU
Phone: 0202 823501
Long established coffee and hot drinks service to business locations, with the attraction of being one that may be started by the franchisee from his/her home.

Number of outlets	62
Set up costs	£7,000
Royalties payable	None
BFA membership?	Associate

Commercial (Brokerage) House

261-269 Ecllesall Road, Sheffield, S11 8NX
Phone: 0742 680476
Financial services based around a computerised system to placing loans and related services.

Number of outlets	30
Set up costs	£18000
Royalties payable	30%
BFA membership?	Applied for

Complete Weed Control Ltd

Langston Priory Mews, Station Rd., Kingham, Oxon OX7 6UW
Phone: 060871 8851
Weed control service to local authorities, government departments,
industry and amenity areas highly regarded by existing franchisees.

Number of outlets	16
Set up costs	£12250
Royalties payable	10%
BFA membership?	No

Condon Alloys

Condon House, Clifton Road, Marton, Blackpool, Lancs FY4 4QA
Phone: 0253 791872
Mobile showroom sales of welding equipment and consumables including
breathing apparatus

Number of outlets	6
Set up costs	£29,000
Royalties payable	None
BFA membership?	No

Copy Cats Ltd

46 Kansas Avenue, Salford Quays, Manchester M5 2GL
Phone: 061-872 4114
Perfume and cosmetics retail outlets from franchisor not known for
providing information very willingly.

Number of outlets	20
Set up costs	£7000
Royalties payable	2%
BFA membership?	No

Country Business Sales

9A Churchgate Street, Southam, Ely, Cambs CB7 5DS
Phone: 0353 723350
Business transfer agency set up in 1986 but with a franchisor who appears reluctant to supply much in the way of information.

Number of outlets	17
Set up costs	£13,950
Royalties payable	10%
BFA membership?	No

Country Properties

41 High Street, Baldock, Herts SG7 5NP
Phone: 0462 896148
Estate agency specialising in village and rural areas and country market towns. Currently operating in part of the Home Counties but preparing to expand.

Number of outlets	18
Set up costs	£25,000 to £40,000
Royalties payable	8%
BFA membership?	Yes

Countrywide Garden Maintenance Services Ltd

164 Stockport Road, Cheadle, Cheshire SK8 2DP
Phone: 061-428 4444
Garden maintenance service serving private houses, business property, office blocks etc.

Number of outlets	14
Set up costs	£18,000
Royalties payable	10%
BFA membership?	Associate

Crimecure

Ivatt Way, Westood Industrial Estate, Peterborough, Cambs PE3 7PB
Phone: 0733 332322.
Installation of burglar alarms, fire alarms, closed circuit television, security lighting and so on. All franchisees are drawn from the electronics trade.

Number of outlets	23
Set up costs	£15,000
Royalties payable	7.5%
BFA membership?	No

Crown Eyeglass PLC

Glenfield Park, Northrop Avenue, Blackburn BB1 5QF
Phone: 0254 51535
Optician service selling low-price spectacles and optical accessories with rapid growth since its launch in 1984.

Number of outlets	100
Set up costs	£23,000
Royalties payable	None
BFA membership?	Yes

Curadraft (GB) Ltd

Delame House, Home Farm, Ardington, Wantage OX12 8PW
Phone: 0235 833022
Prevention of draughts, noise, dust, insect and water penetration using a system which claims to be only 10% of the price of window replacement.

Number of outlets	3
Set up costs	£12,000
Royalties payable	12.5%
BFA membership?	No

Dampco (UK) Ltd

Lythalls Lane, Coventry CV6 6FN
Phone: 0203 687683
Eradication of timber decay and rising damp in domestic and commercial buildings. Existing franchisees suggest that only those from within the building trade should apply.

Number of outlets	10
Set up costs	£10,500
Royalties payable	10%
BFA membership?	No

Dampcure-Woodcure/30 Ltd

Darly House, Cow Lane, Garston, Watford, Herts WD2 6PH
Phone: 0923 663322
Installation of damp courses and treatment of timber with a 30 year guarantee from franchisor established 20 years ago. Previously related to Crimecure/30 - a franchise which has now been sold on to a new franchisor.

Number of outlets	50
Set up costs	£12,500
Royalties payable	15%
BFA membership?	Yes

Data Maid Ltd

47 First Avenue, Deeside Industrial Park, Clwyd CH5 2NH
Phone: 0244 830432
Computer assisted tachograph analysis service to the transport industry run from home by self employed analysts. Not exactly a franchise in the normal sense of the word, but closely related enough to be of interest to franchise hunters.

Number of outlets	105
Set up costs	£11,350
Royalties payable	16
BFA membership?	Early Development Category

Drake International

223 Regent Street, London W1R 1JA
Phone: 01-408 1288
Recruitment consultancy which claims to be the largest "privately owned" such firm in the world, despite being launched only 5 years ago. Provides all types of temporary and permanent staff to all types of businesses.

Number of outlets	22
Set up costs	£40,000
Royalties payable	22%
BFA membership?	No

Duty Driver Ltd

42A Station Road, Twyford, Berks RG10 9NT
Phone: 0734 320200
Chauffeurs to executives to drive the client's car on a part-time basis. Company has grown slowly since its 1985 launch but may now be speeding up.

Number of outlets	5
Set up costs	£12,000 - £20,000
Royalties payable	21%
BFA membership?	Yes

Dyno Electrics

143 Maple Road, Surbiton, Surrey KT6 4BJ
Phone: 01-549 9467
Emergency electrical repair and installation service to home and business customers. Part of the Dyno-Rod group; the high royalties help pay for the name and its extensive advertising.

Number of outlets	25
Set up costs	£12,000
Royalties payable	22.5%
BFA membership?	Yes

Dyno Locks

143 Maple Road, Surbiton, Surrey KT6 4BJ
Phone: 01-549 9467
24 hour emergency lock and complete security service; the smallest of the Dyno group of emergency service franchises.

Number of outlets	23
Set up costs	£12,000
Royalties payable	22.5%
BFA membership?	Yes

Dyno Plumbing

143 Maple Road, Surbiton, Surrey KT6 4BJ
Phone: 01-549 9467
24 hour emergency plumbing repair and installation service in which all the franchisees are qualified plumbers.

Number of outlets	22
Set up costs	£12,000
Royalties payable	22.5%
BFA membership?	Yes

Dyno Rod

143 Maple Road, Surbiton, Surrey, KT6 4BJ
Phone: 01-549 9711
The market leader in drain cleaning and maintenance. Over 25 years experience supporting franchisees through telecommunications, credit control, marketing and training.

Number of outlets	Over 100
Set up costs	£20,000
Royalties payable	22.5%
BFA membership?	Yes

Fixit Tools Ltd

98 Braemar Avenue, South Croydon, Surrey CR2 0QB
Phone: 01-668 4567
Sales of tools and fixings to heating engineers, plumbers, local authorities, plumbers, builders etc from a van. The original company started in 1973 but franchising did not begin until 12 years later.

Number of outlets	10
Set up costs	£12,000
Royalties payable	2%
BFA membership?	No

Fonokleen Services Ltd

VDU House, Old Kiln Lane, Churt, Farnham, Surrey, GU10 2JH
Phone: 0428 713960
Provides a sophisticated valeting service in the telecommunications market. Expert care and specialist know-how is required when cleaning modern electronic equipment for the business sector. This rewarding business service opportunity can be run from home, using a franchisee's own car and appeals to diverse backgrounds.

Number of outlets	6
Set up costs	£7,500
Royalties payable	10%
BFA membership?	No

The Garage Door Company

H and H Domestic Garage Scotland Ltd, Unit 7, Russell Road Industrial Estate, Edinburgh EH11 2NN
Phone: 031-337 9944
Launched in 1959 to supply and fit garage doors, plus repair and replacement of doors, gates, remote controls plus industrial doors and shutters, this company started franchising in 1983. Considered by its franchisees (like so many franchises) to be very hard work.

Number of outlets	10
Set up costs	£19,500
Royalties payable	8.5%
BFA membership?	No

Garden Building Centres

Lye Head, Bewdley, Worcs
Phone: 0299 266361
Retailing and installing conservatories, greenhouses, summerhouses and garden sheds in both modern and traditional design. Ownership of the franchise changed in 1988.

Number of outlets	20
Set up costs	£50,000
Royalties payable	6.5%
BFA membership?	Yes

Grandma Batty's Yorkshire Puddings

Princess Works, Birds Royd Lane, Brighouse, West Yorks
Phone: 0484 714459
Yorkshire pudding restaurants started in 1987. Time will tell if the concept can work nationwide!

Number of outlets	12
Set up costs	£25,000
Royalties payable	2%
BFA membership?	No

Gun-Point Ltd

Thavies Inn House, 3/4 Holborn Circus, London EC1N 2PL
Phone: 01-353 1759
Repointing service for brick and stone properties based on a patented mechanised cleaning system. Claims to be the largest network of specialist repointers in the UK, with all franchisees always having full order books.

Number of outlets	25
Set up costs	£14,500
Royalties payable	12%
BFA membership?	Yes

Hertz Rent a Car

Radnor House, 1272 London Road, London SW16 4XW
Phone: 01-679 1777
Self-drive car and van hire of newish vehicles, from one of best known firms in the field. Has the advantage of being part of an international car hire service.

Number of outlets	92
Set up costs	£50
Royalties payable	10%
BFA membership?	No

Hometune (UK)

77 Mount Ephraim, Tunbridge Wells, Kent TN4 8BS
Phone: 0892 510532
Mobile car engine tuning service which claims to be the best known name
in the business. Franchisees are said to need to be enthusiastic about cars.

Number of outlets	71
Set up costs	£32,000
Royalties payable	17.5%
BFA membership?	Yes

Hurstland Leasing Services Ltd

Hurstland Snailing Lane, Liss, Hampshire, GU33 6HQ
Phone: 04207 443
Hurstland is a franchised dealership network being organised throughout
the U.K. Scope of leasing and contract hire covers heavy and light
commercial vehicles, cars, computers, office equipment, commercial and
industrial plant and equipment. Full Head office operational support will
be given.

Number of outlets	3
Set up costs	£20,000
BFA membership?	Applied for

Intacab

Service House, West Mayne, Basildon, Essex SS15 6RW
Phone: 0268 415891
Franchise operating within the courier, parcel delivery and passenger
transport/taxi markets. The concept is based on the Yellow Cab Company
in Chicago, aiming to cover about two thirds of the UK.

Number of outlets	10
Set up costs	£41,000
Royalties payable	7.5%
BFA membership?	No

Isodan (UK) Ltd

55B Colebrook Road, Royal Tunbridge Wells, Kent TN4 9DP
Phone: 0892 44822
The insulation of external cavity walls. The company (originally started in Denmark) launched in the UK in 1975 and is growing at the rate of about 2 new franchises a year.

Number of outlets	12
Set up costs	£7,500
Royalties payable	None
BFA membership?	No

Kwik Strip

Units 1/2, the 306 Estate, 242 Broomhill Road, Brislington, Bristol BS4 5RA
Phone: 0272 772470 or 716537
Furniture stripping, restoration and renovation franchise run by small family firm, which specialises in taking on husband and wife teams. Ideal for areas packed with older houses.

Number of outlets	23
Set up costs	£9,500
Royalties payable	5%
BFA membership?	Yes

Land and Co Ltd

The Estate House, High Road, Chigwell, Essex IG7 5BJ
Phone: 01-501 2424
Estate agency - claims to be one of the largest in the company, run alongside Link and Co.

Number of outlets	21
Set up costs	£40,000
Royalties payable	12.5%
BFA membership?	Yes

Link and Co Ltd

The Estate House, High Road, Chigwell, Essex IG7 5BJ

Phone: 01-501 5500 Fax: 01-500 4489

FRANCHISOR'S DESCRIPTION: Link and Company offer a comprehensive estate agency franchise based on its sister company, Land and Company Ltd, one of the largest independent estate agents in the UK.

Number of outlets	25
Set up costs	£30,000
Royalties payable	7.5%
BFA membership?	Yes

Lockrite Security

123 Oldham Street, Manchester M4 1LN
Phone: 061-832 6672
Installation of locks, intruder alarms, CCTV to homes and business. The franchisor lays particular stress on keeping initial costs down to a minimum in order to allow an early move into profitability.

Number of outlets	25
Set up costs	£8,000
Royalties payable	10%
BFA membership?	No

Magic Windshields UK

13 Beehive Lane, Gants Hill, Ilford, Essex IG1 3RG
Phone: 01-554 5008
Repair of windscreens, both structurally and cosmetically, developing an idea which has been prevalent in the USA for many years. With the support of insurers the service is supplied for the used car industry, transport generally and the private motorist.

Number of outlets	7
Set up costs	£5,000
Royalties payable	No
BFA membership?	No

M & B Marquees

Morne Court, Burnt Mills Industrial Estate,
Basildon, Essex SS13 1QA
Phone: 0268 728361   Fax: As phone
Hire of marquees, furnishings and services for company functions, weddings, parties, shows, fetes etc. Marquees come in distinctive colours and cause no harm to the environment.

Number of outlets	16
Set up costs	£21,000
Royalties payable	10%
BFA membership?	Associate

Marketing Methods Ltd

1 Buxton Road West, Disley, Stockport, Cheshire SK12 2AF
Phone: 06626 5882
UK network of specialist marketing services for business to business operations. Recognised by the Good Franchise Guide as being particularly highly regarded by its franchisees.

Number of outlets	14
Set up costs	£26,200
Royalties payable	6% to 11.5%
BFA membership?	No

Master Thatchers

Rose Tree Farm, 29 Nine Mile Ride, Finchampstead, Wokingham, Berkshire RG11 4QD
Phone: 0734 734203
Well respected and award winning franchise: the largest thatching company in Europe. The franchise is expanding slowly by design with only two or three franchisees accepted a year.

Number of outlets	21
Set up costs	£15,000
Royalties payable	10%
BFA membership?	Yes

Mixamate Concrete

Beddington Lane, Croydon, Surrey CR9 4QD
Phone: 01-689 5500
Started over ten years ago (which is a long time in franchising) Mixamate vehicles carry cement, aggregate and water, which is mixed fresh at the site, hence avoiding the loss of concrete workability.

Number of outlets	26
Set up costs	from £16,000
Royalties payable	6%
BFA membership?	Yes

Mobile Tuning

The Gate House, Lympne Industrial Park,
Lympne, Nr Hythe, Kent CT21 4LR
Phone: 0303 62419
Mobile engine tuning franchise for all petrol vehicles (second largest such operation in the UK). Unusually this franchisor allows franchisees to start up on a part time basis.

Number of outlets	70
Set up costs	£8,500 to £15,200
Royalties payable	10%
BFA membership?	Yes

Molly Maid UK

Hamilton Road, Slough Trading Estate, Slough, Berks SL1 4QY
Phone: 0753 23388
Light domestic cleaning service established for 12 years. Franchisees are either women, or husband and wife teams. Linked to franchises in Canada and USA.

Number of outlets	34
Set up costs	£10,000
Royalties payable	10%
BFA membership?	Yes

Moseley Financial Consultants Ltd

97 Hagley Road, Edgbaston, B16 8LA
Phone: 021-456 4455
Mortgage brokerage and insurance agency (appointed representatives of Sun Alliance Life) with option to open a shop with capital from franchisor. The company is also involved in the government's right to buy scheme.

Number of outlets	14
Set up costs	£26,500
Royalties payable	None
BFA membership?	No

Multilink (Leasing) Ltd

Hove Park Garage, 132 Old Shoreham Road, Hove, East Sussex BN3 7BD
Phone: 0273 28244
Supplying cars, commercials, specialist bodies, all accessories etc to business user. The outlets are brokers offering part exchange service and advice on all makes of cars rather than just one.

Number of outlets	20
Set up costs	£21,000
Royalties payable	30% gross profit
BFA membership?	No

Mundays

The Bellbourne, 103 High Street, sher, Surrey, T10 9QE
Phone: 0372 67272
Legal Services for people starting in franchising.

Multi-Marque Vehicle Contracts Ltd

The Old Vicarage, 25 Church Street, Uttoxeter, Staffs
Phone: 0889 567383
Specialists in advising small to medium sized businesses on vehicle
leasing and contract hire, and fleet management. The franchisor promises
no capital is tied up in stock, there are no bad debts and few overheads.

Number of outlets	6
Set up costs	£7,190
Royalties payable	5%
BFA membership?	Applied for

National Car Care Ltd.

Wilmson House, Southend Road, Woodford Green, Essex, IG8 8HJ
Phone: 01-551 4911
This company have launched over 40 franchises during 1989. It
encompasses Total Car Care: - Mobile Valeting, Specialised Vehicle
protection and Sun Roof Fitting. During 1990 National Car Care will be
adding additional profit centres to those already mentioned and these
opportunities are available to all franchisees.

Set up costs	£7,000
Royalties payable	1st yr-£150 p/m, 2nd yr £200 p/m, thereafter 2.5%
BFA membership?	Early Development Category

National Security

Britannia House, Lea Crane Road, Luton, Beds LU3 1RJ
Phone: 0582 459336
Supplier of security systems and alarms, from a franchisor linked with The Bath Doctor. Started in 1987 and growing very rapidly.

Number of outlets	27
Set up costs	£14,000
Royalties payable	12.5%
BFA membership?	No

National Slimming Centres

3 Trinity, 161 Old Christchurch Road., Bournemouth, Dorset BH1 1JU
Phone: 0202 25233
Safe medically controlled weight loss.

Number of outlets	38
Set up costs	£45,000
Royalties payable	10%
BFA membership?	No

Newlook Bath Services

Oaklands, Dorstone, Hereford HR3 6AR
Phone: 0981 550297
Repair and renovation of baths, sinks, bidets etc including chip repair, removal of stains and re-enamelling, from a franchisor established over 20 years ago.

Number of outlets	11
Set up costs	£12,500
Royalties payable	10-20%
BFA membership?	No

Novus Windscreen Repair

11 Darwin House, Dudley Innovation Centre, Dudley Road, Kingswinford, West Midlands DY6 8XZ
Phone: 0384 401860
Windscreen repair company offering a mobile repair service to vehicle owners. The franchisor claims over 3000 outlets in 30 countries, with a product that satisfies the standards of all insurance companies and all EC countries.

Number of outlets	51
Set up costs	£7,000
Royalties payable	
BFA membership?	Yes

O'Corrain Heraldry

22 Dunlop Industrial Estate, Bangor, Co Down BT19 2QY
Phone: 0247 451036
Research and manufacture of hand painted heraldic shields with family histories. The shields are produced by one factory for all franchisees, and dramatic growth of turnover is being predicted for the next year.

Number of outlets	12
Set up costs	£12,000
Royalties payable	None
BFA membership?	No

Odd-Jobs (UK) Ltd

5 Bridge Street, Macclesfield SK11 6EG
Phone: 0625 610765
Cleaning agency specialising in the domestic market, which can be run by a franchisee from home. Also takes in domestic gardening and some light commercial work.

Number of outlets	2
Set up costs	£7,500
Royalties payable	6%
BFA membership?	Early
Development Category	

Open Fire Centres Ltd.

Cattespoole Mill, Tardebigge, Nr Bromsgrove, Worcestershire B60 1LZ
Phone: 021-445 5550
Retail fireplace and fireside accessory shops, which has started in the
Midlands in the past two years but is looking to expand into the rest of the
UK.

Number of outlets	4
Set up costs	£22,000
Royalties payable	7%
BFA membership?	Yes

PIP Printing

Black Arrow House, 2 Chandos Road, London, NW10 6NF
Phone: 01-965 0700
Success is based on the sound and well proven principle of high quality
support to franchisees. The Business, which centres on successful outside
sales effort, centres on offset lithographic printing and the high-tech world
of computerised artwork and typesetting systems. Royalty includes 2.5%
advertising fund.

Number of outlets	60
Set up costs	£90,000
Royalties payable	10%
BFA membership?	Yes

Practical Used Car Rental

137/145 High Street, Bordesley, Birmingham B12 0JU
Phone: 021-772 8599
One of the most famous add-on franchises, (over 100 outlets now
operating) offering car and van hire integrating with services already
provided by firms in the motor trade. In addition to the profits from the
actual franchise the franchisor suggests extra petrol sales, car sales and
workshop revenue through the additional people visiting the site.

Number of outlets	112
Set up costs	£18,000 minimum
Royalties payable	8%
BFA membership?	Yes

Professional Appearance Services (Pasclean)

1 Queen Square, Bath, Avon BA1 2HE
Phone: 0225 312756
Car valeting, contract cleaning and carpet and upholstery cleaning services. This franchise is designed to start as an owner-operator business, and then grow as the owner takes on staff and becomes a manager of the operation.

Number of outlets	29
Set up costs	£9,850
Royalties payable	8% plus £250
	occasional additional royalty
BFA membership?	Yes

Protoplas

1 Carn Industrial Estate, Portadown, N Ireland BT63 5RN
Phone: 0762 333193
A "technology transfer license" particularly aimed at the handyman turned franchisee. It centres on a plastic repair service for automotive industrial, domestic and farm use.

Number of outlets	12
Set up costs	£15,000
Royalties payable	None
BFA membership?	No

Quattro Seal

Suite 2, New Mansion House, Wellington Road South, Stockport SK1 3UA
Phone: 061-480 4991
Window and door sealing system that eliminates water, draughts, dust penetration and reduces noise. The system has been developed under a government grant, and claims to be the only one of its type.

Number of outlets	80
Set up costs	£9,950
Royalties payable	None
BFA membership?	No

Recognition Express

PO Box 7, Rugby Road, Hinckley, Leicestershire LE10 2NE
Phone: 0455 38133
Manufacture and sale of name badges, interior and exterior signs, vehicle livery and corporate trophies and awards for other businesses. The franchise was launched in 1979, and formerly known as Badgeman.

Number of outlets	17
Set up costs	£22,500
Royalties payable	12.5%
BFA membership?	Yes

Safeclean

Delmae House, Home Farm, Ardington, Oxon OX12 8PN
Phone: 0235 833022
Home cleaning plus stain removal of carpets, uphostery, curtains on site.
This franchise can be run from the franchisees own home. In addition to
the UK outlets there are also franchises in Ireland and Belgium.

Number of outlets	80
Set up costs	£10,500
Royalties payable	10%
BFA membership?	Yes

Saks Hairdressing

57 Coniscliffe Road, Darlington, Co Durham DL3 7EH
Phone: 0325 380333
Hair salon franchise which at present is concentrated mostly in the North
East, but is expected to take in the rest of the country in the next few years.

Number of outlets	16
Set up costs	£30,000 - £50,000
Royalties payable	10%
BFA membership?	Yes

Service Master

308 Melton Road, Leicester LE4 7SL
Phone: 0533 610761
Long established but still expanding on site carpet and upholstery cleaning
and furnishing repair, which is linked to the Merry Maids Domestic
Cleaning Service.

Number of outlets	260
Set up costs	£7,500 - £10,250
Royalties payable	7% - 10%
BFA membership?	Yes

Silver Shield Windscreens

Wheler Road, off Humber Road, Whitley, Coventry CV3 4UA
Phone: 0203 307755
Windscreen and body glass replacement specialist.   Customers with emergency problems call a freephone number which is diverted to the nearest franchisee.

Number of outlets	65
Set up costs	£25,000 - £50,000
Royalties payable	10%
BFA membership?	Yes

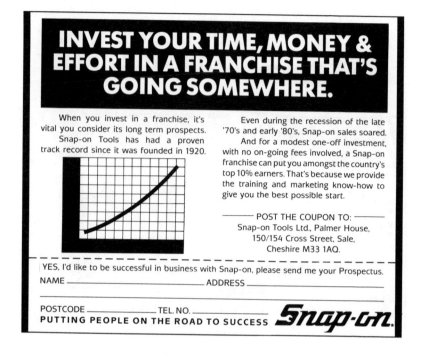
Snap On Tools Ltd

Palmeer House, 150-154 Cross Street, Sale, Cheshire, M33 1AQ
Phone: 061 969 0126
The franchise consists of visiting garages and similar outlets, selling a range of company supplied products for the automotive trade.

Number of outlets	364
Set up costs	£36,000 approx
Royalties payable	None
BFA membership?	Yes

Snappy Tomato Pizza (UK) Ltd

17 Mercia Business Village, Torwood Close, Westwood Business Park, Coventry CV4 8HX
Phone: 0203 466647
Take away and home delivery pizza operation linked to an American operation - this is one of the very few food franchises available at £50,000 or less.

Number of outlets	13
Set up costs	£50,000
Royalties payable	8%
BFA membership?	No

Stained Glass Overlay

SGO UK Ltd, PO Box 65, Norwich, Norfolk NR6 6EJ
Phone: 0608 485454
Part of the Anglian Windows Group, specialists in the field of decorative glass and mirrors. Launched in 1986 the franchisor is looking to take on half a dozen franchisees a year.

Number of outlets	9
Set up costs	£25,000
Royalties payable	10%
BFA membership?	Associate

Suds Mobile Car Valet

Hine House, Randlesdown Road, London SE6 3BT
Phone: 01-695 5127
Car valet service from a fully-equipped van, with the aim of franchisees building from a one van to a multi-van business over a few years.

Number of outlets	12
Set up costs	£5995
Royalties payable	2.5% plus £125 per month
BFA membership?	No

Swinton Insurance

6 Great Marlborough Street, Manchester M1 5SW
Phone: 061-236 1222
High Street Insurance Specialist with what is described as a "revolutionary concept in selling insurance". Just over half of the outlets are franchised - the rest being company owned. Despite the high number expansion is continuing.

Number of outlets	390
Set up costs	£30,000
Royalties payable	6%
BFA membership?	Yes

The Maids Ltd,

Global House, 8-10 High Street, Sutton, Surrey SM1 1HN
Phone: 01-643 0138
Home cleaning service (including normal cleaning plus carpet, upholstery and curtain cleaning) provided by uniformed teams of cleaners. Much of the work (which excludes weekend working) is for regular customers.

Number of outlets	15
Set up costs	£35,000
Royalties payable	10%
BFA membership?	Yes

TNT Parcel Office

TNT House, Abeles Way, Atherston, Warwickshire CV9 2RY
Phone: 0827 303030
Add on franchise for the receipt of packages for through transmission via the TNT service worldwide.

Number of outlets	460
Set up costs	£5,000
Royalties payable	None
BFA membership?	Yes

Toasty Kitchens

2 Castle Street, Salisbury, SP1 1BB
Phone: 0722 27456
Mobile catering units offering toasted sandwiches sold at shows and events throughout the country. Obviously a franchise whose income is greatly affected by the seasons, and the weather.

Number of outlets	11
Set up costs	£8,250
Royalty	£78 per month
BFA membership?	No

Trafalgar Cleaning Chemicals

Unit 4 Gillman's Industrial Estate, Natts Lane, Billingshurst, West Sussex RH14 9EZ
Phone: 0403 815111
The supply of cleaning chemicals and equipment to the motor and transport industries. The franchise currently centres on the south of England, the Midlands and the North West, but is expanding into other areas.

Number of outlets	31
Set up costs	£5,900
Royalties payable	2%
BFA membership?	Application pending

Transform Solid Wood Replacement

280 Balham High Road, London, SW17 7AL
Phone: 01-767 1272
Offering a comprehensive franchise providing complete marketing, advertising, selling, and technical support to the franchisee. They supply any size door in solid wood in a choice of 600 different finishes to face lift existing kitchens and bedrooms.

Number of outlets	12
Set up costs	£8,500
Royalties payable	None
BFA membership?	No

Trust Parts Ltd

Unit 7, Groundwell Industrial Estate, Crompton Road, Swindon, Wilts SN2 5AY

Phone: 0793 723749

The market leader in sales of engineering and workshop supplies. The franchisee works as a one-man-band, selling these products from a specially designed van carrying over 900 different lines.

Number of outlets	57
Set up costs	£12,000
Royalties payable	5%
BFA membership?	Associate

Tune-Up Ltd

23 High Street, Bagshot, Surrey GU19 5AE
Phone: 0276 51199
Diagnostic and engine tuning services carried out at the customers home or work place. Tune-Up is unusual in that the overwhelming majority of its shareholders are themselves franchisees - which gives an interesting extra guarantee of the interests of the franchisees being maintained.

Number of outlets	80
Set up costs	£12,500
Royalties payable	10%
BFA membership?	Associate

Uticolor (GB) Ltd

19-20 Grosvenor Street, London W1X 9FD
Phone: 01-965 6869
Vinyl and leather repair and recolouring service. The franchisor stresses the high level of selectivity involved in picking franchisees. Most franchisees are currently based in the south east and Midlands.

Number of outlets	21
Set up costs	£12,000
Royalties payable	10%
BFA membership?	Yes

VDU Techclean Services Ltd

VDU House, Old Kiln Lane, Churt, Farnham, Surrey, GU10 2JH
VDU Techclean provides a highly sophisticated valeting service of computer and high tech equipment on a regular basis to the business sector. Special care and know-how is needed when handling sensitive technology. No computer experience required as on-site training is given. Can be run from home.

Number of outlets	35
Set up costs	£12,500
Royalties payable	10%
BFA membership?	No

Ventrolla Ltd

51 Tower Street, Harrogate, North Yorks HG1 1HS
Phone: 0423 67004
Draughtproofing and window renovation service which is promoted as a low cost alternative to double glazing. The franchise which was set up in 1983 is owned by the Laird Group Plc.

Number of outlets	16
Set up costs	£15,000
Royalties payable	10%
BFA membership?	Associate

Video Round UK Ltd

Suite 2, New Mansion House, Wellington Road South, Stockport SK1 3UA
Phone: 061-429 9939
Home video rental franchise which launched in 1987 and is planning to expand at a very, very fast rate. A unique feature is that the franchisor promises the franchisee 300 guaranteed customers.

Number of outlets	21
Set up costs	£4,750
Royalties payable	None
BFA membership?	No

Vista Travel

2 The Walk, 128 High Street, Billericay, Essex
Phone: 0277 657011
Travel agents specialising in cruises, low cost flights and independent travel. Franchisees are recommended to have travel trade experience.

Number of outlets	7
Set up costs	£40,000
Royalties payable	1%
BFA membership?	No

Votre Beaute (Franchise) Ltd

Cattespoole Mill, Tardebigge, Nr Bromsgrove, Worcestershire B60 1LZ
Phone: 021-445 5550
A relative newcomer to the franchising scene, this franchise offers a combination of beauty centre, cosmetics retail and hairdressing salon. Previous hairdressing experience is not required by potential franchisees.

Number of outlets	2
Set up costs	£30,000
Royalties payable	10%
BFA membership?	Yes

Weightguard Slimming Clubs

Henlow Grange Health Farm, Henlow, Beds SG16 6DP
Phone: 0462 811111
Slimming clubs offer a diet using natural foods, initially for weight loss. At present the franchise operates exclusively in South East England, but it is considered to be viable for anywhere in the UK.

Number of outlets	58
Set up costs	£1350
Royalties payable	17%
BFA membership?	No

USEFUL NAMES, ADDRESSES AND PUBLICATIONS

Associations and companies

The British Franchise Association
Franchise Chambers,
75A Bell Street,
Henley-on-Thames,
Oxfordshire RG9 2BD
Tel: 0491 578049

The International Franchise Association
1025 Connecticut Avenue,
Suite 1005,
Washington, DC 200236,
USA

European Franchise Federation
77 Mount Ephraim,
Tunbridge Wells,
Kent TN4 8BS
Tel: 0892 510532

Franchise Development Services Ltd,
Castle House,
Norwich NR2 1PJ
Tel: 0603 620301

Franchise World
James House,
37 Nottingham Road,
London SW17 7EA
Tel: 01 767 1371

Institute of Marketing
Moor Hall,
Cookham,
Maidenhead,
Berkshire SL6 9HQ
Tel: 06285 24922

The Association of British Factors
147 Fleet Street,
London EC4A 2BU
Tel: 01 353 1213

Association of Invoice Factors
Jordan House,
47 Brunswick Place,
London N1 6EE
Tel: 01 623 8462

British Insurance Brokers Association
10 Bevis Marks,
London EC3A 7NT
Tel: 01 623 9043

The Chartered Association of Certified Accountants
29 Lincoln's Inn Fields,
London EC2A 3EE
Tel: 01 242 6855

The Chartered Institute of Management Accountants
63 Portland Place,
London W1N 6AB
Tel: 01 637 2311

BANKS

Bank of Scotland Plc
57-60 Haymarket,
London SW1Y 4QY
Tel: 01 925 0499

Barclays Bank Plc
Marketing Department,
54 Lombard Street,
London EC3P 3AH

Clydesdale Bank Plc
30 St. Vincent Street,
Glasgow G1 2HL
Tel: 041 248 7070

Lloyds Bank Plc
Franchise Unit,
Small Business Service,
71 Lombard Street,
London EC3P 3BS
Tel: 01 626 1500

Midland Bank Plc
Mariner House,
Pepys Street,
London EC3N 4DA
Tel: 01 260 8859

National Westminster Bank Plc
Franchise Section,
Small Business Sector,
Commercial Banking Services,
Finsbury Court,
101-117 Finsbury Pavement,
London EC2A 1EH

The Royal Bank of Scotland Plc
42 Islington High Street,
London N1 8XL
Tel: 01 833 2121

The Royal Bank of Scotland Plc
42 St. Andrew Square,
Edinburgh EH2 2YE
Tel: 031 556 8555

TSB Scotland Plc
Henry Duncan House,
120 George Street,
Edinburgh EH2 4TS

PUBLICATIONS AND FURTHER READING

Daily Mail Book of Running a Small Business, Hawthorne, Harmony, 1989

Financial Management for the Small Business, 2nd Ed., Barrow, Kogan Page, 1988

Franchise Magazine, The, FDS Ltd, Castle House, Norwich NR2 1PJ

Franchise Newsletter, The, Monthly, Franchise Publications Ltd

Franchise World, Qtrly, Franchise World, James House, 37 Nottingham Rd., London SW17 7EA

Franchising, NatWest Small Business Bookshelf, Pitman, 1989

Franchising Report, The, Euromonitor Publications

Good Franchise Guide, The, Attwood & Hough, Kogan Page, 1988

Guide to Franchising, A, Mendelsohn, 5th Ed., Pergamon, 1987

Law and Practice of Franchising, Mendelsohn, Franchise Publications, 1982

Marketing in Small Businesses, Kenny & Dyson, Routledge, 1989

Taking up a Franchise, 5th Ed., Barrow & Golzen, Kogan Page, 1989

The U.K. Franchise Directory, 5th Ed., FDS Ltd, 1988

INDEX